COMMUNION BEFORE CONFIRMATION?

The report of the General Synod Board of Education Working Party on Christian Initiation and Participation in the Eucharist, Chaired by the Bishop of Knaresborough.

CIO PUBLISHING
Church House, Dean's Yard, London SW1P 3N2

ISBN 0 7151 9035 0

Published 1985 for the General Synod Board of Education by CIO Publishing

Printed in England by Burgess & Son (Abingdon) Ltd.

Contents

Foreword from the Bishop of Knaresborough

As Chairman of the Working Party which has produced this report, I express my public thanks to all its Members for the major contribution which each and every one of them has made. Expecting some sizeable disagreements on the major issues concerned, we found ourselves quickly moving reflectively and prayerfully to the consensus which the Report expresses and which we hope the Church will accept and act upon. It will involve a major change in the pastoral practice of any parish which wishes to implement its recommendations and it will need careful consideration. It is, however, my hope and belief that when implemented prayerfully and responsibly it will make a major contribution to the nurture and consequent growth of many of the Church's young people, a matter which must be of the deepest concern to us all. We commit it with confidence, therefore, to the Church.

+John Knaresborough

Members of the Working Party

CHAIRMAN
The Rt Rev. John Dennis (The Bishop of Knaresborough)

The Rt Rev. Alec Graham (The Bishop of Newcastle)

Dr Robert Bocock (Lecturer in Sociology, The Open University)

The Rev. Canon Colin Buchanan (Principal, St John's College, Nottingham; Member of General Synod during the life of this Working Party; Bishop Designate of Aston)

The Rev. Dr John Frederick (Rector of Blechingley)

Miss Marjorie Freeman (Children's Officer, Board of Education) (from February 1985)

Mrs Penny Granger (Member of General Synod during the life of this Working Party)

The Rev. Barry Miller (West Midlands College of Higher Education; formerly Children's Officer, Board of Education)

Dr Elizabeth Moberly (Ridley Hall, Cambridge; member of the Orthodox Church)

The Rev. Robert Teare (Rector of Holy Trinity and St John in the Soke with St Martin, Winnall, Winchester; Member of General Synod during the life of this Working Party)

Mrs Helena Wildblood (formerly Diocesan Youth Officer, Bristol)

*The Rev. Prof. Stephen Sykes (Van Mildert Professor of Divinity, Durham)

SECRETARY
The Rev. David Isaac (National Youth Officer, Board of Education)

*Due to outside pressures, Professor Sykes had to relinquish membership of the Working Party after three meetings. We are grateful for the major contribution he had already made to our thinking.

The Working Party presented its unanimous report to the Board of Education in June 1985.

Background and Terms of Reference

After the General Synod debate in February 1983 on the motion proposed by the diocese of Winchester, the Board of Education, encouraged by the Standing Committee, reconstituted an existing Working Party with the following *Terms of Reference*:

Taking note of the 1976 Resolution of General Synod, to review:

(a) the admission of baptised persons to Communion before Confirmation and experiments that have been undertaken in this field. The Working Party was asked to continue the work of evaluating and monitoring such experiments;

(b) the theological, sociological and historical aspects of the rite of Confirmation in the Church of England;

(c) the place of Confirmation in parish life especially in relation to changes in liturgy and pastoral care;

(d) ways forward that combine the best educational practice with particular theological approaches and to recommend, if it thinks fit, a particular solution or solutions to the problems arising in respect of differing practices;

(e) the importance of a continuing framework of training for the Christian life.

taking account of practices in the Anglican Communion and other Churches.

The Working Party was asked to respond in detail to the Board of Education and suggest how the Board might most appropriately take the matter further, in the context of the Synod's request to the Standing Committee arising out of the February 1983 debate.

CHAPTER 1

The Shape of the Report

1.1 'Confirmation before Communion' has been the customary practice in the Church of England long enough to become enshrined in popular consciousness as 'the way things are'. 'And there shall none be admitted to the Holy Communion, until such time as he be confirmed, or be ready and desirous to be confirmed'.[1] In our examination of the issue we have tried to discover if the way things are is the way they have to be. We have concluded unanimously that it is open to the Church of England to alter its accepted practice, if it so desires. We begin our report with some statements clarifying the position we take with regard to Baptism and the nature of tradition, and examine the process which led to the Reformation understanding of Baptism, Confirmation and Eucharistic participation in the Church of England.

Christian Initiation and nurture in the faith have theological, sociological, psychological and educational dimensions and we have tried to indicate some of the questions raised by these disciplines. The need for change is suggested by factors both of principle and of pastoral care and it may hardly be surprising that we have found similar ferment and unease in many parts of the worldwide Church. Practice in the Church of England with regard to admission to Communion before Confirmation has developed significantly in recent years; we have tried to note something of what is currently happening in the dioceses and to reflect upon some of the implications of making a change. Our report concludes with some recommendations and suggestions for a way forward which we hope will be of assistance to those who must debate on these issues, both nationally and locally.

THE DEBATE SO FAR

1.2 The events which led up to the present report are as follows. In 1969 the 'Ely' Commission was appointed to consider questions concerning Christian initiation, and it reported in *Christian Initiation: Birth and Growth in the Christian Society* (CIO, 1971). One of the central conclusions it drew was that Baptism is complete sacramental initiation, and it recommended that Baptism should be viewed as a sufficient basis for admitting children to Communion, prior to Confirmation. Whereas the task of the present working party has been to focus primarily on the issue of admission to Communion before Confirmation, we have taken note of the Ely Report's recommendations relating to the administration of Baptism. These related to:

(a) the conditions under which infants should be accepted for Baptism;

(b) whether or not the Church of England should have an official service for thanksgiving (or some variant on thanksgiving) for a new-born child.

In respect of (a), the Synod in February 1974 affirmed that Baptism was for infants whose parents were 'willing and able' to make the requisite promises; but in November 1976 the Synod accepted by a narrow majority a motion which had come from the Southwell diocese in the course of the initiation debate:

> That this Synod . . . . . desires that there should be a re-examination of the conditions upon which infants are accepted for Baptism.

This matter was referred by the Standing Committee to Bishop Knapp-Fisher, who wrote a one-man report on the issue; but the report has never been brought back to the Synod, so the motion above remains the Synod's last statement on the issue.

In respect of (b), the reference to the dioceses included a question about services for new-born children. As a result, the Synod accepted the desirability of a service of thanksgiving after the birth of a child: the Liturgical Commission drafted one, the Synod revised and authorised it, and it is now part of the Alternative Service Book.

1.3 The Ely report was debated in a preliminary way in Synod in July 1971, and was then delayed for over two years whilst a Standing Committee report, digesting and summarising the argument and recommendations, was prepared by the Rev. Peter Cornwell. This report was debated in February 1974, and the Synod then passed a motion, which included the statement that the Synod 'accepts the principle that full sacramental participation within the Church may precede a mature profession of faith', and which referred the matter to the dioceses to ask whether they would support this principle, either by simply admitting children to Communion before Confirmation or by uniting the laying on of hands (or anointing) with infant Baptism, so as to keep something like the traditional sequence.

From Spring 1974 to Spring 1976 this was debated in the dioceses. Their response to the main proposal was lukewarm and this, in July 1976, gave the General Synod reason to think there was insufficient support to proceed with a change in admission to Communion. The voting on the motion, tabled but not recommended by the Standing Committee, was as follows:

	AYES	NOES
Bishops	17	27
Clergy	83	132
Laity	86	112

When this was defeated, the Synod passed a following motion encouraging bishops to use the discretion they have under Canon B.27 to permit Confirmation at a somewhat younger age than has been traditional, 'in consultation with their Synods'. It is not clear that Canon B.27 does in fact confer any such discretion on bishops and the working party has not heard of any bishop consulting with his Synod to this end.

1.4 Nevertheless, the issue did not rest there. Various quasi-official 'experiments' had already started, and could not easily be stopped. The Synod voting of July 1976 showed a very sizeable minority wishing to approve a change without an overwhelming mandate from the dioceses, and in many parishes pressures were building up.

Some evidence of this is contained elsewhere in this report (see para. 7.6). It was in Winchester diocese that the issue first broke surface again synodically. The diocesan synod passed a motion in 1980 asking for the change, and this came on to the General Synod agenda in November 1981 in this form:

> That this Synod requests the Standing Committee to review the General Synod's Resolution of July 1976, disallowing the admission of baptised persons to the Holy Communion followed at a later stage by Confirmation with a view, in the light of the growing demand for such an option, to permitting the introduction of this change in certain dioceses for a period of twelve years, as a pilot experiment.

When the motion was tabled, the Board of Education set up a small working party, under the chairmanship of the Bishop of Knaresborough, to provide background information and research in advance of the synod debate, and this first met early in 1982.

The motion itself did not reach the agenda for debate until February

1983, and it was then moved by the Rev. Robert Teare on behalf of the Winchester Diocesan Synod. Certain objections were made; that the 'growing demand' was not proven; that naming 'certain dioceses' would be invidious; and that prescribing the outcome of the review was to pre-empt the process of reviewing. Thus an amendment by Canon Michael Hodge, to omit all words after '. . . . . later stage by Confirmation', was carried by 143 votes to 124. The amended motion was then carried by 228 votes to 104.

1.5 The Standing Committee, in handling the request of Synod, conveyed to the Board of Education the desirability of enlarging its existing working party, and this was duly done. The former working party held an already planned consultation of representatives of parishes engaged in unofficial changes of practice in June 1983, and then received its additional members early in 1984. The members of the renewed working party have found that their 'review' has taken them unanimously into recommending changes of practice beyond the limited experimentation sought in the Winchester motion.

---

[1] 1662 Prayer Book: Order of Confirmation rubric.

CHAPTER 2

Scripture, the Early Church and Later Developments

2.1 Baptism with water in the name of the Trinity is a sign of God's gift in Christ and marks the point of entry into the Church universal, the Christian community which is both within and beyond time and space. While this Report by its nature focuses on the place of the individual in the local congregation, it must be proclaimed that Baptism admits to the communion and fellowship of the Catholic Church and that everything that follows must be seen against that. It also needs to be emphasised that Baptism, giving entry into the new Covenant, like circumcision which afforded entry into the old Covenant, is unrepeatable. In both cases the right of entry is 'once for all'.

2.2 On the relationship between Baptism and the practice of Communion, the New Testament evidence is significant, though slight. Acts 2, 41–42 indicates that those baptised are admitted to the 'breaking of bread': the assumption of I Cor. 10 is that the recipients of the letter have been baptised and are sharing in eucharistic fellowship. Early indications are given too in the *Didache* and in the *Apology* of Justin Martyr that Baptism admits to participation in Communion, though without reference to age.

2.3 Such evidence as there is in Scripture for the Baptism of children has a cumulative strength. There is the Old Testament background of infant circumcision as the way of entering the Covenant community; and a contemporary Jewish background to the New Testament which probably included the baptism of proselytes and their families. Within the New Testament itself it is clear that Baptism came at the very beginning of Christian life. The varied instances of households being baptised (Acts 10; Acts 16; I Cor. 1) help to substantiate the case. Children are regarded as being *within* the Church, not merely hearers or catechumens. The passage in Mark 10 (about Jesus welcoming the children) may not have much relevance here, but the mention of children in Acts 2. 38,39 and the open-ended reference to the children of one believing parent in I Cor. 7. 14 must be taken into account. In addition to the argument from later tradition, there is a biblical case for infant Baptism.

2.4 Although the New Testament does not enlarge upon the place of children and, especially, young children, in the life of the Church, we can confidently affirm that they were there. The difficulty of tracing a firm connection between their presence in the company of the New Testament people of God and their sacramental participation has certain implications.

2.4.1 First, that the biblical evidence is not decisive. Some early patristic evidence points to infant reception of Communion, but there is no explicit scriptural precedent for this practice.

2.4.2 Second, any attempt to extract evidence from Scripture concerning the constitutive elements of Christian Initiation and qualification for participation in the Eucharist must recognise that the evidence only concerns adults. We should be wary of regarding children as a case for special theological treatment. Only one Baptism is given a theology in the New Testament. To make anything different of the Baptism of children is to risk making it something other than Baptism.

2.4.3 Third, the issue of a post-baptismal laying-on-of-hands or anointing must be raised. It is an open question as to whether it should be viewed as an original element in initiation but, since it was used in the succeeding centuries and has sometimes been regarded as an essential constituent of a 'primitive integrated rite' (which later 'disintegrated'), it deserves some consideration. There are many instances in the Acts of the Apostles where there is no mention of such a rite (Acts 2. 41; 8. 35; 10. 48; 16. 33; 18. 8) and it is entirely absent from the whole Pauline corpus. The early Church itself does not provide us with the clear 'integrated' starting point that has sometimes been affirmed. In the early East (e.g. in the *Didache,* Ignatius of Antioch and authors through to the fourth century) and in the second-century West (e.g. Justin) there is no mention of such a post-baptismal rite. It is only with Tertullian and Hippolytus, at the dawn of the third century, that the rite first appears as a complex amalgam of various elements. We do not see it, therefore, as a primitive norm, but, rather, as a historical development which was later reversed. It is not normative in the same sense as in the universality of water-baptism in the New Testament accounts.

2.5 Before looking at the specifically Anglican tradition, we must therefore shed any presuppositions arising from the developments in the Initiation rite as a result of practical rather than theological reasons. The related issues of Baptism, the gift of the Spirit, faith, and Eucharistic participation are issues of concern for Scripture because they are all elements in what together makes for membership of Christ's body, the Church. Each, therefore, is to be considered in its own right, quite apart from the later considerations of what might be appropriate to various age groups within the Church.

2.6 The earliest known examples of the Baptism and Eucharistic participation of children support the view that child candidates were regarded as being no less capable of initiation than were adults. In the early third-century *Apostolic Tradition* of Hippolytus, children are baptised at the same service as adults, and implicitly have the same things done to them, including the episcopal imposition of hands and anointing, before, presumably, participating in the Eucharist. Only at one point is there any indication that children are to be treated differently. '..... Baptise the little ones first. All those who can speak for themselves. As for those who cannot speak for themselves, their parents or someone from their family shall speak for them.....'[1] Recognising that, for the early Church, the profession of a sponsor committed the one baptised as surely as a personal profession, we may note that no distinction is made between the content of child or adult Baptism, and the same benefits are apparently conferred.

Certainly, by the time of Cyprian (d. 259) infant Communion was established as well as infant Baptism in its fullness. In Cyprian we find an already developed theology of the practice. The completing of John 3. 5 ('..... unless one is born of water and the Spirit, he cannot enter the kingdom of God .....') with John 6. 53 ('..... unless you eat the flesh of the son of man and drink his blood, you have no life in you') establishes what is necessary for participation in the Christian community.[2] A child who receives Baptism shares the divine gift so given. It affords entry into membership of the Church, which thereafter depends on continued participation in the Eucharist. To be capable of receiving Baptism is to be capable of receiving Communion.

2.7 In the New Testament, the life of the baptised was expressed by participation in the common life of the Church of which the celebration of the Eucharist was a central feature. On the day of Pentecost about three thousand souls were added to the Christian community by receiving Peter's word and accepting Baptism; 'And they devoted themselves to the apostles' teaching and fellowship, to the breaking of bread and the prayers' (Acts 2. 41f). Acts 2. 46 repeats the reference to the centrality of the breaking of bread in the life of the community. For St Paul the sharing in the Lord's Supper should be a sign for unity, not a cause for division. Whenever Christians 'assemble as a Church' (I Cor. 11. 18) the eucharistic action is, by implication, expected (c.f. Paul's criticism 'when you meet together, it is not the Lord's Supper that you eat' I Cor. 11. 20). The thrust of Paul's argument is that the Lord's Supper must be shared in such a way that everyone should be enabled to participate properly (e.g. I Cor. 11. 22 which warns against a less than total sharing of the bread and wine).

2.8 While it is silent on baptismal practice with regard to children, the New Testament knows nothing of the exclusion of those who are baptised from the central meal of the Church.

2.9 The biblical doctrine of the covenant between God and his people further strengthens this argument. In the inauguration of the Old and New Covenants God's initiative and commitment are prior to human response and this is reflected in the signs which characterise admission to and continuance in the covenants. Circumcision and Baptism are the means of entry into the covenant communities. One of the strands which may be discerned in the Jewish passover and Christian Eucharist is the renewal of that Covenant relationship. This relationship with God is understood as being communal in nature, while not ignoring the need for a response from individuals appropriate to their capabilities.

2.10 From this understanding of the relationship between the two sacraments of the New Covenant there would appear to be nothing, in principle, to debar those who have been admitted into the covenant community from sharing fully in the sign by which its corporate relationship with God is continually affirmed.

2.11 Augustine (354–430) reflects extensively on infants and the Eucharist. Part of the outcome of this reflection was to make the infant the model of the perfect subject for the sacraments, both as a reminder of the total helplessness of the human condition; and as exemplifying the ideal pre- or non-rational approach to the mystery of the Eucharist revealed in John 6. However, this is not to make the infant a special case on the grounds of its innocency. Rather, all that is to be found in an adult is to be found present and operative in the infant: 'It is the physical weakness of the baby that makes it seem innocent, not the quality of its inner life'.[3] For this reason the infant stands in need of sacramental aid. The nature and benefits of the Baptism administered to infants are, therefore, no different from those which adults may receive.

2.12 However, Augustine's doctrine of Original Sin, by encouraging the Baptism of infants as early as possible, contributed to the drifting apart of Baptism, laying on of hands by the bishop, and admission to Communion.

2.13 During the medieval period, Baptism, Confirmation and admission to Communion were occurring as separate events in the Western Church. Key factors in determining this pattern were:—

(a) the practical impossibility of having the Bishop as the minister of Baptism with a laying-on of hands (and anointing),[4] joined with the increasing emphasis on the need to ensure that infants were baptised as soon as possible so that they should not die in original sin. The result was an interval of at least seven years between Baptism and Confirmation.

(b) an increasingly 'realistic' view of the Eucharist, together with a scrupulosity in the administration of the consecrated elements resulting in the withdrawal of the chalice from the laity and the exclusion of children from the reception of Communion.

These facts were later given theological justification. In the words of J.D.C. Fisher, what the Western Church had done was to say, in effect:

> Infants are not now presented for Confirmation: therefore infants do not need Confirmation; the Church normally gives Confirmation to adolescents:

> therefore the grace conveyed by Confirmation must be the spiritual strength particularly needed by those entering adolescence.

Similarly,

> Infants are not allowed to receive Communion; the Church cannot be supposed to have excluded them from Communion without good cause: therefore infants have no need of sacramental Communion, and the grace which they receive in Baptism must be supposed to suffice until they are of an age to commit actual sin.[5]

In finally abolishing infant Communion, the Council of Trent gave the justification that infants regenerated through Baptism and lacking the use of reason were under no obligation to receive the sacramental communion of the Eucharist.[6] Communion, then, was the food of adults; their spiritual nourishment was necessary from the age of discretion when the ability to commit sin stood them in need of the grace received in Holy Communion.

Confirmation had not been seen as a necessary precondition for admission to Holy Communion. Archbishop Peckham's regulation issued at the Council of Lambeth in 1281 (barring admission to those not confirmed or not reasonably prevented from receiving Confirmation) was but a matter of discipline directed against the 'damnable negligence' of parents content only to have their children baptised. By then, the Church had been communicating unconfirmed infants and adults for centuries.

2.14 As inheritors of the Anglican tradition, we have received a pattern of initiation practice which, as it developed through history, gradually made Confirmation a prerequisite of admission to Communion and theologised each stage of the process. The early stages of the process are well-illustrated by the contribution of Bishop Faustus of Riez who, in the fifth century, asked why Confirmation after Baptism should be necessary.[7] His answer was, 'So far as I can see, we have not obtained everything from the font, if after the font we still need the addition of something new'.[8] Baptism, then, he deduced, needed something to complete it, and Faustus equated the gift conveyed by Confirmation with the gift of the Spirit initially outpoured at Pentecost. By the time of the 1938 Report, *Doctrine in the Church of England,* the Archbishops' Commission on Doctrine would state, 'it is evidently appropriate that the rite wherein the gift of the Holy Spirit is bestowed in its fullness should normally precede admission to participation in the rite which expresses the completeness of Church-membership and of its obligations'.[9] The Commission's conclusion may be seen as but another stage in the theological sanctioning of 'de facto' processes. This is not to say that it is necessarily wrong! These processes occur within the life of the Church; theology must recognise pastoral expediency and the need to interpret in the best way what is or has become, a muddle in practice. Yet such interpretations may also embody a number of red herrings, particularly arising from the idea that Confirmation completes the giving of the Spirit to the individual, and is to be given a fixed place in the sequence of Baptism—Confirmation—Holy Communion.

2.15 We must therefore look away from the theological justification of developments in the Initiation rites to the evidence of Scripture on the relationship between Baptism and the gift of the Spirit. Here we see that certain passages do at first sight give support to those who argue that the episcopal imposition of hands and/or anointing convey the gift of the Holy Spirit. In Acts 8. 14–17 Samaritan converts 'baptised in the name of the Lord Jesus' receive the Spirit when the apostles Peter and John lay hands upon them. Similarly, in Acts 19. 1–7, after the Baptism 'in the name of the Lord Jesus' of some of John's former disciples, 'when Paul had laid his hands upon them, the Holy Spirit came on them'. But this is scarcely Confirmation in the modern sense. For the author of these passages in Acts it would be true to say that to have received the Spirit is to have the mark of the Christian, but the Spirit may come in a variety of ways. In Acts 10. 47 the fact of the Spirit's outpouring independent of any human action is made the ground for the Baptism of Cornelius and his household. In Acts 2. 37ff. Peter declares repentance and Baptism to be the way not only to the forgiveness of sins, but to the reception of the gift of the Holy Spirit. Speaking on the day of Pentecost, Peter makes no reference to the laying-on of hands. It is a change of heart and Baptism which are all important. To describe Baptism as a Christ-event for the forgiveness of sins, and Confirmation as the continuance of the Pentecost-experience is to read 'into' Scripture, not out of it.

Certainly for St Paul, there can be no division of gifts received in Baptism and in a Spirit-related rite. Rather, 'by one Spirit we were all baptised into one body' (I Cor. 12. 13). Individuals should expect to have individual gifts of the Holy Spirit, but there can be no ritualised means of conveying these gifts. Rather, of primary importance is the 'fruit of the Spirit' (Gal. 5. 22) which is the common characteristic of the community of the faithful, the heirs of God and fellow-heirs with Christ who live by the law of the Spirit of life in Jesus Christ—the whole of Romans 8 is a glorious confusion between life in Christ and life in the

Spirit which defies any neat distinctions. For Paul, then, what the Spirit does cannot be separated from the work of God in Baptism. To be baptised is to be made a member of Christ's body; members of that body express their common life sharing in the one loaf; and they are to live in the Spirit who has set them free and given them sonship in Christ.

Further references can be found elsewhere in the New Testament. Hebrews 6. 2 is of no help: 'baptismon', a plural, is probably better taken to refer to unspecified acts of ablution than to Christian Baptism (Heb. 9. 10), and 'the laying on of hands' is capable of wide reference. I John 2. 20–27 refers to an 'anointing' (charisma) by the Holy One, and the New English Bible goes so far as to translate this as 'initiation'. Any ritual seems unlikely, though the term might find its currency by reference to contemporary mystery cults. It is helpful to consider its root—'christos', the Anointed one (a root shared with the terms Messiah and Christ). To be 'anointed', whether or not in the context of a Church rite, is to be made a member of the messianic community. It will entail sharing the messianic gifts of that community and these may be expressed as gifts or attributes of the Spirit. They remain the corporate gifts of the community. The individual who is initiated participates with them—he does not receive them as his own; rather he receives the Spirit who works in the Church. To be a member of the Church, then, is to share in the Spirit of the messianic community. It would not seem possible to be a member and not share in the Spirit. Therefore, it is necessary to be critical in our approach to Confirmation rites which make reference to the giving of the Spirit. Particular use is made in various rites of Isaiah 11. 2ff. with its reference to the Messiah's gifts:

> . . . . . the spirit of the Lord shall rest upon him,
> the spirit of truth and understanding,
> the spirit of counsel and might,
> the spirit of knowledge and the fear of the Lord.

To be a fellow-heir with Christ is to share in his gifts. It may be correct for the Church to pray for an individual's increase in these gifts. It is difficult to see how it can be denied that they exist in unconfirmed but baptised members of the Church.

2.16 The difficulties encountered in the above discussion have a bearing on the practice of Churches in which Baptism and Confirmation are administered separately. Origen could say 'Through the laying-on of hands the Holy Spirit was given in Baptism'.[10] Even so Origen recognises that God cannot be tied to set rites: '. . . . . I find in the divine Scriptures several catechumens who were held worthy of the Holy Spirit and that others after receiving baptism were unworthy of the grace of the Holy Spirit. . . . . Cornelius was a catechumen and before he came to the water he desired to receive the Holy Spirit. Simon (Magus) had received baptism but he was refused the gift of the Holy Spirit because he approached the grace with hypocrisy'.[11]

2.17 An attempt has been made in this chapter to touch upon some of the more important biblical and patristic passages which bear upon our theme. Such an attempt in so short a compass is bound to yield an unsatisfactory result. Nevertheless, enough has been included to convey an impression of the complexity of the material which we have inherited from the first five Christian centuries. The biblical evidence leads most easily to the conclusion that in the Church of the first century there was a wide diversity of practice and of understanding, particularly regarding the imposition of hands in Christian Initiation. Streeter applied his quotation from *Alice in Wonderland,* 'Everyone has won, and all shall have prizes' to the hypothesis of a primitive diversity in Christian institutions; it may be equally well applied to a primitive diversity in our field as well. It is easy to find in the Scriptures, and in the early centuries too, precedents for a wide variety of later developments. We have ourselves pursued a line which we are convinced makes consistent sense. It is, however, different from some which would have been popular a decade or two ago, in as much as it does not follow the paths mapped out by Puller, Mason and Dix, nor does it (unlike the Preface to the Order of Confirmation in the 1928 Prayer Book) regard as normative for the subsequent life of the Church the passage in Acts 8 concerning the spread of Christianity to Samaria. While we have made some reference to developments in the Medieval period, the treatment of our theme in the sixteenth century demands more detailed attention and to that we now turn.

---

[1] Hippolytus, *Apostolic Tradition* 21 (in Grove Liturgical Study No. 8).

[2] Cyprian, *Ad Quirinium* III, 25. Cited in D. Holeton *Infant Communion—Then and Now* (Grove Liturgical Study No. 27), p. 5.

[3] Augustine, *Ex in Ps* 54, 24, 3311, 1; *Confession* 1, vii; II cited in *ibid,* p. 6.

[4] The signing of the cross which the oil of chrism came to be seen as the 'form' of Confirmation rather than the related imposition of hands.

[5] Cited in J.D.C. Fisher, *Christian Initiation: Baptism in the Medieval West, A Study in the Disintegration of the primitive Rite of Initiation* (1965), p. 139.

[6] *Ibid,* p. 106.

[7] This is the first known use of the term 'confirmation'. Faustus's sermon became established in the False Decretals and, attributed to the fourth century Pope Melchrades, was read by a number of leading medieval authorities, including Gratian and Aquinas.

[8] Fisher, *Baptism in the Medieval West,* op. cit., p. 125.
[9] The Report of the Commission on Christian Doctrine (1938), p. 189.
[10] Cited in *ibid,* p. 186.
[11] Origen, *Hom. in Numeros,* iii, I.

CHAPTER 3

The Reformation Understanding

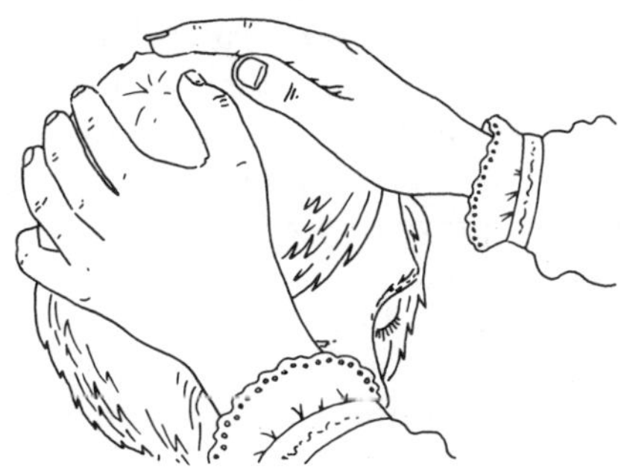

3.1 The Working Party benefited from a long memorandum prepared by a Durham research student, the Rev. Martin Jackson, about the Reformers' understanding of the relationship between Baptism, Confirmation, and admission to Communion. This has been appended to this report (Appendix 4). The chapter that now follows sketches the outline of the argument at the points where it bears most closely on the age and conditions for admission to Baptism.

3.2 The Reformers retained infant Baptism as universally required, though they might be thought to have been somewhat skimpy in their defences of it in the Articles and Prayer Book. They also retained Confirmation, but apparently as a rite which arose from (in the words of Article XXV) 'the corrupt following of the Apostles' and which they felt able to reform for their own pastoral purposes.

3.3 Cranmer stated that the conferring of the Spirit was not now the function of Confirmation, but he located the gift of the Spirit sacramentally in Baptism, and even then only under the right conditions. He provided that catechising should precede Confirmation—indeed should be part of the rite—and thus made fairly clear that it was the ability to answer for themselves which marked the candidates' part in the rite, and that the bishop came to 'approve' or 'confirm' them. In the rite itself, the old Confirmation prayer (drawn from Is. 11) had called on God to 'send down from heaven upon them thy Holy Ghost', but in 1552 this was changed to 'strengthen them with thy Holy Ghost'. The rite was *not* now initiatory, not even a 'booster', but a rite about continuance in Grace. Similarly, the formula at the ministering of Confirmation to the individual candidate was changed from the Sarum 'I sign thee with the sign of the cross and I confirm thee with the chrism of salvation. In the name . . . . .' In 1549 it became 'I sign you with the sign of the cross and I lay my hand upon you . . . . .'—a text which simply described the outward action but gave it no significance. And in 1552 it became 'Defend, O Lord, this thy child . . . . .'—a text which has no 'formula' character to it whatsoever, but could be prayed by any one Christian for any other on any occasion. The outward sign was also changing (as the texts display). In Sarum it was signing with oil but without the imposition of hands; in 1549 it became a signing without oil, but with the addition of the laying on of hands; and in 1552 it became the laying on of hands only. Cranmer might say in the post-confirmation prayer 'upon whom (after the example of thy holy apostles) we have now laid our hands to certify them . . . . .', and could even have claimed he had restored the apostolic sign. However, he was not suggesting that Acts 8. 14–17 (about the Samaritans) provided a basis for interpreting the significance of Confirmation, and the meaning of the laying on of hands he presented in the most general and unsacramental way possible.

3.4 Nevertheless Cranmer incorporated the old provision of Archbishop Peckham into his new Confirmation rubric that 'there shall none be admitted to the Holy Communion, until such time as he can say the Catechism, and be confirmed'. The emphasis here is much more upon the understanding of the faith implied in the catechism than in the undergoing of the rite of Confirmation. The Reformers inherited a notion that some ability to answer for oneself was a necessary condition for admission to Communion, and they systematised the notion to suit their own presuppositions. In particular, they viewed learning the faith as the necessary deliverance from the superstition in which they had themselves been brought up, and inevitably placed a premium upon the ability to respond to catechisms. They wrote further very lengthy catechisms to supplement the official provision, and this reinforces the sense that their initiatory sequence was: Baptism—instruction—Communion. Confirmation was the certificate of instruction.

3.5 Various other factors followed the authorisation of the 1552 Prayer Book. In Mary's reign the exiles in Frankfurt were ready to give up Confirmation under pressure from the more puritan element, as a 'thing indifferent'. Calvin, in his *Commentaries* on Acts and in the *Institutes,* presented an early church history which looked like Cranmer's pattern of Baptism—instruction (Confirmation)—admission to Communion, and this gave great authority to the practice. The Puritans kept up great pressure against the rite, and its defenders, such as Jewel and Whitgift, were able to plead only that it was not ungodly, not that it was a universally necessary sacrament. The administration of Confirmation was no more thorough than it had been in the Middle Ages. It seems that from the sixteenth century to the nineteenth the great preponderance of Anglican communicants were admitted to Communion not on the basis of being confirmed, but of having been baptised and having received some minimal instruction from the parochial incumbent. This was self-evidently so in, for instance, the American colonies in the eighteenth century, but seems to have been little different in many parts of England. Ordination candidates were often confirmed the night before their ordination. The 'age of discretion' was between 13 and 16; Bishops were supposed to do confirmation tours once every three years to gather in the candidates of the whole triennium, but this was very often neglected.

3.6 The 1662 Prayer Book retained most of the Reformers' emphases, though it removed the Catechism from within the Confirmation rite. It also made it clear in a slightly different way from before that it was the instruction rather than the rite which was crucial for reception of Communion; the Confirmation rubric now read '. . . . . until such time as he be confirmed or be ready and desirous of being confirmed'. It also required Confirmation for those baptised in 'riper years'—a question which had not arisen in 1552. The Prayer Book set the pattern whereby in the nineteenth century a more intensively 'pastoral' use of Confirmation arose, which in turn fixed in the minds of very large numbers of Anglicans the conviction that it was the unshakeable Anglican tradition and ruling that Confirmation was an absolute precondition for receiving Communion. This, by the 1880s, led to the theological insistence that Confirmation was the completion of sacramental initiation.

3.7 We must now consider the role of tradition in Anglican theological understanding. Did the Reformers fasten a particular tradition upon us for ever, albeit one open to changing understandings, or did they provide a principle of reformation which would encourage us to look critically at what we have inherited?

CHAPTER 4

The Nature of Tradition in the Church of England

4.1 'Tradition' has been defined as 'anything bound up with and continuing in the life of a family, community etc'. (*Chambers' Dictionary*). To pay attention to the 'tradition', then, is to recognise the value of belief and practice established in the past, that which is, literally, 'given over' from one generation to another. Elements in the tradition may be deemed fixed and unalterable, to be accepted as established by all subsequent generations. Canon A5 of the 1969 Canons of the Church of England takes the view that the Church's doctrine may be established from a certain corpus of material:

> The doctrine of the Church of England is grounded in the Holy Scriptures, and in such teachings of the ancient Fathers and Councils of the Church as are agreeable to the said Scriptures. In particular such doctrine is to be found in the Thirty-Nine Articles of Religion, the Book of Common Prayer, and the Ordinals.

4.2 Canon A5 specifies the area of the tradition in which true doctrine is to be found. The Reformation formularies need not be expected to express the whole of the truth, for only of Scripture can it be said that it 'containeth all things necessary to salvation'.[1] Yet they may be expected to focus our attention within the wider limits of Catholic faith and practice; they express the Anglican tradition, not as the exclusive vehicle of God's truth, but as agreeable to true doctrine and the Word of God.[2]

4.3 Thus it becomes clear that the 'tradition' contains both Christian truths fixed for all time and also elements of understanding which evolve from age to age. All valid Christian tradition must arise from the life of the Church, faithful to the Scriptures. But as it grows it may express the Church's faith in new ways. In the words of the Worship and Doctrine Measure, the Church of England 'professes the faith uniquely revealed in the Holy Scriptures and set forth in the Catholic creeds, which faith the Church is called upon to proclaim afresh in each generation. Led by the Holy Spirit, it has borne witness to Christian truth in its historic formularies, the Thirty-Nine Articles of Religion, the Book of Common Prayer and the Ordering of Bishops, Priests and Deacons . . . . .'

Clergy and other office-holders are required to affirm their loyalty to this 'inheritance of faith' as their 'inspiration and guidance under God'. In doing so they affirm not an inheritance of faith fixed as the sole expression of Christian truth but one which has been a means of conveying the truth in the past and the present. The primary aim is to bring 'the grace and truth of Christ to this generation', and in this task the formularies inspire and guide as examples of the fulfilment of that task.

4.4 The Book of Common Prayer and other Formularies have, therefore, a dual role of guiding and inspiring. They are not to be taken lightly if we are to be faithful to the Anglican tradition. But how far are they to be taken as normative in describing the practice of the Church? In this, two considerations are relevant:

4.4.1 Article XX, 'Of the Authority of the Church', affirms the Church's 'power to decree Rites or Ceremonies' which are not 'contrary to God's Word written'. This allows the ordaining of rites within the Book of Common Prayer which might have no explicit Scriptural basis. When, therefore, we assess the basis of the BCP rites, we need to remember the Article's rider that anything without a scriptural basis may not be enforced 'to be believed for the necessity of Salvation'. Anything without that basis is at most a matter of discipline, not of doctrine.

4.4.2 Canons A2 and A3 state the Thirty-Nine Articles and the BCP to be 'agreeable to the Word of God'. Yet it may be also that these latter do not work out the full implications of their use of Scripture, implications which might lead us to formulate new disciplines.

4.5 It is clear, from this understanding of the nature of tradition in the Church of England that changes in matters of discipline are both possible and, sometimes, necessary.

---

[1] *Articles of Religion,* VI.
[2] cf Canons A2 and A3.

CHAPTER 5

The Wider Context of Society

5.1 CONCEPTIONS OF CHILDHOOD

5.1.1 Conceptions of childhood are not constant, nor are they natural. They vary from one historical period to another and from one cultural group to another. For example, children in the eighteenth and nineteenth centuries were used to sweep chimneys, to work on farms, down mines, and in factories. In some parts of the world today, children are used for quite important work tasks.

5.1.2 Many children brought up in Britain in the first half of this century were told: 'Children should be seen and not heard.' It is a measure of the changes which have occurred in many people's conceptions of childhood since the end of the 1940s that such a statement is now hardly ever heard. Far from being told that adults do not want to hear them, children born in the last few decades are encouraged to speak as early as possible, and to talk with other people as much as possible. Such changes in our general ideas about children have recently come to affect the role of young children in the life of the Church.

5.1.3 The social changes which have emerged in the last decade in the role of young children in family discussions, and family life generally, are now having their effects in the central family service of the Church, the Eucharist. Some children now express a desire to receive Communion. Adults find it increasingly difficult to find satisfactory reasons to explain why they cannot do so.

5.1.4 Whilst it is true that sociologists cannot solve theological problems, they may be able to shed some light upon why a particular problem arises within the life of an organisation such as a Church at a particular time and place. A sociological perspective may also help in understanding some of the difficulties of adaptation to change by a specific organisation such as the Church of England. There are some sociological points to be borne in mind about contemporary English society, and about growing up in it, which affect the consideration of the admission of children to Communion before Confirmation.

5.2 CONTEMPORARY ENGLISH SOCIETY

5.2.1 Any comparative analysis of modern, urban, industrial societies with past and present rural, agricultural ones will show England in the 1980s to be a society changed in many features. Of these, the most important for changing our understanding of church membership is that modern English society is best described as 'pluralist' rather than either as 'traditional' or 'totalitarian'. In other words, there is some variety of political, economic, and cultural institutions, including a range of religious bodies and traditions which are allowed, or encouraged, to exist in such a society. Traditional societies have never allowed or encouraged such a variety; nor do modern totalitarian regimes. In these societies there is one central religion, or political ideology, which is held to be sufficient for all purposes.[1] Pluralism has its effects upon the socialisation of young children in a church, because it is ultimately impossible to insulate children from the variety of religious and non-religious ideas to be found in a modern society. Under these conditions religion becomes a matter of individual choice.

5.2.2 The social position of the Church of England reflects an earlier historical era in which attempts were made to contain everyone within one Church in the newly-emergent nation state being built by the Tudors. Other modern states in Europe share this characteristic of having an established Church. The United States, importantly, does not.[2] In this respect England and Scotland are less pluralist than the United States, but are influenced by its mass media, so that there is absorbed the idea of freedom to choose from a variety of religious viewpoints. This makes more and more young people critical of the role of the Church of England in the life of the nation and of the state. Pluralist societies produce an ever-increasing emphasis upon the freedom of the individual to choose—to choose among brands of toothpaste, ice cream, shampoos, cars, clothes, music, politics, religions and philosophies.[3] There are supermarkets for various goods, and 'supermarkets' for religions and philosophies, as can be seen in the many bookshops catering for people with an interest in these ideas.

Many people, including some parents, teachers, and clergy, find it hard to see how a religion can be legitimately imposed upon children. There are those who think that an individual should be allowed, and educated to exercise, free choice in a religion, as they are with regard to their occupations and marriage partners. Just as arranged marriages seem inappropriate to those living in modern pluralist cultures, so parental choice of a religion can seem equally illegitimate.[4]

5.2.3 Modern parents face a new situation, especially if they are both practising Christians in the Church of England, and aware of the pluralism in the modern world in which their own children are growing up. On the one hand they wish to give their children some religious background within their own Church; equally, on the other hand, they do not wish to seem to have indoctrinated their children—something they may have felt happened to themselves, or which their children may think when they reach the age of maturity.

5.2.4 This wider cultural situation, especially that of American pluralism, influences adolescents in England and is probably a factor in causing the drop-out of many young teenagers from the Church of England. Another such factor is that Confirmation, often administered to people in their early teens, does not lead to a marked increase in responsibility for the young person. Yet to join a congregation which then does not offer a young member a significant task, or tasks, to perform, appears to the young people themselves to convey the message that the Church does not value what they may have to offer. Such tasks could be anything from mending chairs or tables, to helping with younger members of the Church, to assisting in services, to paying amounts of money to the Church. Young people might well value being able to contribute something of their time, skills, energy, and money after affirming their membership of the Church. If the Church of England appears not to value them, then they may go to another religious organisation which does give them a set of tasks to perform and thus seems to the young themselves to value them more highly.

5.3 RELIGIOUS ORGANISATIONS

5.3.1 Sociologists have devoted a considerable amount of work to the sociology of religious organisations—Churches, denominations, and sects. One important factor which distinguishes the way in which sociologists define a 'Church'-type organisation as distinct from a 'sect' is precisely over the method of entry. In a 'Church', membership is typically by birth into it; in a 'sect'-type of religious organisation membership is by adult conversion.[5] Some 'sects' continue to recruit new adult members over the years. Others cease making many new adult converts and become what sociologists refer to as 'denominations': members are born into the group and few new converts are made. 'Churches', however, remain distinct as a sociological category from 'denominations', even though the latter are based largely upon members who are born into them.[6] Those religious organisations which retain episcopacy and a sacramental system are termed 'Churches' by many sociologists, and they may be 'Established Churches' in a particular nation state, as is the case with the Church of England.[7]

5.3.2 The twentieth century has seen the growth of many sects and cults, especially in the United States and North Western Europe, including Britain.[8] One major reason for this growth of sects has been that young adults can join a sect as an act of individual self-assertion and identity-seeking. This is much more congruent with the ideology of consumer free choice which has come to be the central feature of the mass culture of western societies. A variety of religious sects and cults compete for the attention of people, and those which market themselves successfully, by meeting the 'real' needs of considerable numbers, grow and build up recruits, often from among young people who were brought up in a main Church or denomination of Christianity. One of the major attractions of joining a sect is to assert that there is something unique about oneself, or one's group. This helps in the 'collective search for identity'—an identity which members imagine is created, or at least chosen, by themselves and not handed to them by parents, teachers and clergy.[9] Thus it could be said that, in an important sense, many sects are protest movements against the main churches and denominations of Western societies. They are a protest against a world that is laid on for the young by parents and earlier generations. As the sociologist Erving Goffman wrote:

> Whenever we look at a social establishment we find ..... that participants decline in some way to accept the official view of what they should be putting into and getting out of the organization, and behind this, of what sort of self and world they are to accept for themselves ..... Whenever worlds are laid on, underlives develop.[10]

5.3.3 These trends pose problems for Churches which initiate infants into membership in Baptism. On the one hand they face a falling-away of members as young people attempt to find their own identity in new religious or political movements. On the other, they recognise the need to provide an opportunity, in early adulthood or later in life, for an affirmation of a more than nominal membership. The increasing trend towards providing opportunity for re-affirmation of baptismal promises, at Easter and at other times, is an indication of this.

5.3.4 From this kind of sociological point of view it is possible to see that enabling children to receive Communion after Baptism but before being confirmed, would leave Confirmation available for use at a much later stage in the life cycle. Were there thought to be no important theological reasons for not admitting baptised children to Communion, then retaining Confirmation for a later occasion as a rite of individual affirmation of faith might go some way to meet the new sociological situation outlined above in which people feel they wish to make an individual choice about the religion they espouse.

5.4 RITES OF PASSAGE

5.4.1 Within social anthropology, work has been done on the ritualisation of movement from one social status to another—from being unmarried to being socially recognised as a potential, or actual, mother or father; from being a child to being an adult; from being involved in everyday activity to being involved in 'sacred' activities, as in Ordination. These rituals were termed collectively 'rites of passage' by the anthropologist Van Gennep (1960). It is possible to distinguish between the general term, 'rites of passage', and particular types of such rites, as in the example of 'life-cycle rituals'. These life-cycle rituals include thanksgiving for a birth; naming a baby; the passage from childhood to adulthood; becoming socially recognised as a parent; leaving this world and passing into the next one. There is also another type of ritual marking a passage from one social position to another; the 'civic ritual'[11] around the process of joining and leaving a group, or a modern organisation, such as becoming the Mayor of a town or city; receiving a gift upon retirement from an employing organisation; graduating in universities.

5.4.2 The rituals of what is now called 'Christian Initiation' include both of these two types, and some confusion results in practice from this mix. Some clergy and laity emphasise the aspects of Baptism and Confirmation as rituals which mark joining an organisation, a Church, and which sharply distinguish members from non-members. Others emphasise the life-cycle ritual aspect: that is, an element of the 'folk-religion' of ordinary people in a parish. This is the kind of ritual found in pre-literate, non-industrial, societies, in which a new-born infant is named, and accepted as belonging to the wider community. These two aspects of initiation are more of a problem in an established Church such as the Church of England, because everyone in a parish is, or was, regarded as able to use Baptism for their new-born infants. This reflected a time when most families lived in villages or small parishes, and would either be churchgoers or well known to others who were. This kind of assumption can no longer be made in many parishes today, and so there is now more concern with the nurture of those who are baptised into the Church of England.

5.4.3 Many pre-literate, non-industrial, societies did not have any period of adolescence or childhood as these have emerged in modern industrial societies, but they had rituals which marked a passage from being socially regarded as a child to being an adult (for example, being able to fight, or to become a parent). These rituals were frequently found to be carried out at puberty for boys and girls.[12]

5.4.4 Within the recent history of the Anglican Church in East and Central Africa there has been an interesting case of a missionary bishop, Bishop Lucas (Bishop of Masasi, Tanzania, 1926–1944) attempting to 'christianise' the local, indigenous rites of passage at puberty by introducing Confirmation at this point in the life-cycle rituals of the Anglican Church. These 'tribal' rites existed for both boys and girls; in the case of boys who had reached puberty the rites included circumcision and this continued even after the participants were baptised Christians.[13]

5.4.5 In such a rural agricultural society, based upon complex kinship networks, there is a marked absence of a period of adolescence, and of adolescent rebellion, such as is found in a modern, urban, industrial society. For this reason it is not possible to argue that such rites of passage at puberty 'ought' to be retained in a modern context. The move from childhood to adulthood now lasts some years, and is a period of major choices for the young—choice of educational process; choice of occupation, if one can be found; choice of a partner; choice of a 'life-style'; choice of a moral, political, and religious viewpoint, if any.[14] This contrasts with traditional and tribal societies in which no such choices faced the young. They were often provided with a marriage partner; they would usually follow in their father's or mother's footsteps in terms of work; and typically they would accept the faith of their ancestors.

5.4.6 In a modern society such as England, therefore, Confirmation cannot easily come at any clearly-marked moment of transition from one phase of life to another. In modern England, Confirmation often comes before the young person is able intellectually or emotionally to make an adult choice. In retrospect, it is often seen by the young people themselves as being an immature decision. Rather, it can be experienced as having been something into which they were manipulated, and this can leave them with feelings of resentment.

---

[1] B. Turner, *Religion and Social Theory* (1983), p. 200.
[2] D. Martin, *A General Theory of Secularisation* (1978).
[3] P. Berger, *The Social Reality of Religion* (1969).
[4] M. Mead, *Coming of Age in Samoa* (1928, 1963).
[5] E. Troelstch, *The Social Teaching of the Christian Churches* (1931).
[6] R. Niebuhr, *The Social Sources of Denominationalism* (1959).
[7] M. Yinger, *The Scientific Study of Religion* (1970).
[8] B. Wilson, Ed. *Patterns of Sectarianism, Organisations, and Ideology in Social and Religious Movements* (1967).
[9] O. Klapp, *Collective Search for Identity* (1969).
[10] E. Goffman, *Asylums* (1961).
[11] R. Bocock, *Ritual in Industrial Society* (1974).
[12] A. Van Gennep, *Rites de Passage* (1960).
[13] W. Lucas, *The Christian Approach to Non-Christian Customs in Christianity and Native Rites* (1928).
[14] See Appendix 3.

CHAPTER 6

Educational and Psychological Perspectives on Christian Growth

6.1 The Eucharist is the great prayer and act of thanksgiving of the Church of God and can, as such, be entered into by all present, whether or not they receive Communion. However, the sharing of Holy Communion lies at the heart of the Eucharist and it is at this point that many children feel left out.

6.2 Understandably, therefore, there is a strong request from many children to be allowed to receive communion. The eight-year-old who 'cornered' the Bishop after a Confirmation service and demanded to know why he would not confirm her was not actually interested in Confirmation as such, but was asking to be allowed to develop her relationship with Jesus in Holy Communion. Three years previously she had called going up to the altar rail 'saying hallo to Jesus', and was now clear about her desire to share in communion with Jesus and the rest of the Church family.

6.3 The insights of this child and many others do not show an intellectual ability to explain the meaning of Communion. Their understanding is often at a more direct, affective level. A quite young child is capable of perceiving both the naturalness and the 'specialness' of sharing in the bread and wine. It is a sharing of food and drink, and yet it is something much more which is to be felt and experienced rather than explained. A child can know this. A child can also feel a sense of exclusion from something which is obviously of importance to adults and which binds them together, leaving her or him out, and seeming to deny his or her awareness of love and of belonging. 'I love Jesus *now*', one child said, 'so why *can't* I share?' Many adults would often feel glad to understand as much as some of their children, and are just as incapable of putting their understanding into words!

6.4 Indeed the level of the significance of the sacrament varies from adult to adult, and from one occasion to another for the same adult. We must surely accept the understanding of the child or young person, the mentally handicapped or emotionally disturbed person, as being capable of the same variations and levels of meaning and richness. Indeed the very nature of a sacrament contains within it different levels of meaning, and analysis is not the best way to appreciate its fullness. The associations, unconscious as well as conscious, which surround the imagery and symbolic functions, are made up of many strands of experience and knowledge, and the very fact that ordinary material things (bread and wine) are used means that there are associations and experiences for everyone, old and young. It is interesting to note that, from the evidence of a modest survey carried out by Dr Marion Smith (Roehampton Institute of Higher Education) and the Rev. Barry Miller in 1984, symbols are usually imbued with several layers of meaning for people.[1] Our understanding of the meaning of a symbol develops as life proceeds. The attempt, however well-intentioned, to convey the accumulated meaning of a symbol in a didactic manner may well prevent any real understanding of such a symbol being gained.

6.5 Indeed, the last twenty years have seen a conscious effort in Christian education to help children, in particular, to explore some of these experiences of everyday life within a Christian context.

6.6 In the mid-1960s the Board of Education pioneered new approaches in education programmes for the Christian Community. *Alive in God's World* was the Board's response to the research of Ronald Goldman. Goldman based his work on Piaget and produced a developmental pattern of religious understanding. One aspect of his thesis was that the Bible stories and their concepts were beyond the understanding of young children. His own answer towards a new approach in Religious Education was the production of a series of books and workcards on a thematic basis.

6.6 The Wadderton Group, established by the Board of Education, was familiar with the experiential learning approach which was being used in other areas of the Board's work, and it produced a thematic experiential learning 'package'. As it turned out, this material was to be used as much in day schools as by parish groups. The material had the child-centred approach of other areas of the school curriculum and leaders of children's groups in churches said 'How good to have material to help the children to explore the whole of their lives in a Christian way, to bind together the secular and the religious, to allow for feeling as well as thinking, and learning through doing as well as by talking!' Other publishing houses began to produce a similar material and over the past fifteen years the message of 'not too much and not too soon' began to be heard and understood by clergy and Sunday School teachers. Now the Church has found itself hoist with its own petard. Those who have been advocating the admission of children to the eucharist at an early age have been told, 'Children do not understand these difficult concepts . . . . . and *you* said so!'

6.7 More recently there has emerged an awakened awareness of the need for Christians to be aware of their roots. Children (and adults) tend to be less knowledgeable about Biblical context and the teaching of the Church, and there are initiatives to help them explore such truths without denying the insights and experience of the last decades.

6.8 The current debate about admission to Communion is, to some extent, a review of the Church's attitude to children. *The Child in the Church* report and its sequel *Understanding Christian Nurture* have tried to explore the importance of *all* learning experiences which may develop *faith* (not simply religious understanding) in children.

6.9 The latter report sets out to explore how 'Christian nurture' is similar to, and yet very different from the process of secular education. The distinctions are important in helping the church to form a policy for education. First we need to understand the 'new' term: Christian Nurture. The report defines it as 'a Christian rationale for a Christian learning about Christian faith leading to deeper faith'.[2] One of the important concepts associated with both nurture and secular education is that of 'critical openness'. The report seeks to show that 'critical openness' comes from an understanding of the Christian faith itself. It is an approach which is derived from the demands made by the Gospel about the way we live. In our modern pluralist society it is important that the Christian faith should be 'critically open both towards itself and towards its fellow (or rival) world views'.[3]

6.10 With this as a central concept the report lists the main distinctive features of Christian Nurture. The first is that 'Christian nurture is based on the hypothesis that Christianity is true and can be seen to be yet more true'.[4] This does not mean that the task is to demonstrate 'proofs' that the Christian faith is true. Rather, Christians are encouraged to be engaged in a quest which reveals 'more truths'. The theme of quest and exploration recalls the aims of the *Alive in God's World* material; that children might discover faith rather than learn about faith. It is important, therefore, that this exploration should take place in the faith community. This is the context for Christian Nurture. It follows from this, and from the view that critical openness is a characteristic of that community, that children and adults are fellow-learners. They may indeed be at different stages of faith but it may be false to suggest the stage of development of faith is related solely to chronological age. The work of James Fowler and others[5] have helped to open up new ways of thinking about faith development which has many implications for Christian nurture. As definitions of adulthood and maturity are called into question, there are renewed demands to *listen* to children and young people and for adults to benefit from learning from and with the younger members of the church.

> The Church that does not accept children unconditionally into its fellowship is depriving those children of what is rightfully theirs, but the deprivation such a church will itself suffer is far more grave.[6]

6.11 In speaking of psychological development, it is sometimes assumed that all significant growth takes place during the first few years of life, and the middle to end years of the second decade of life are socially recognised as marking the transition to adulthood. However, it is in fact highly misleading to assume that no significant development takes place after the end of the second decade. Changes and development are a constant feature of adult life. Most popularly, some recognition is nowadays given to the mid-life crisis. This—like the turmoil of adolescence—is but one of the developmental crises that any person may expect to encounter during the course of his or her life.

6.12 A developmental crisis is not necessarily a crisis in the popular sense of the word. Rather it marks a critical transition from one stage of development to the next. External events may accompany or contribute to adult development. Such events would include marriage, childbirth, a new job, or unemployment. Irrespective of the particular external events that may occur, there is also an ongoing need for inner change. Apart from this polarity of inner and outer, it must also be noted that some changes are predictable while others are unexpected, such as redundancy or the premature death of a spouse.

6.13 Typical developmental crises, or 'passages', may be described in such terms as those of Gail Sheehy (1974). After 18 comes the period of 'Pulling Up Roots'. This is followed by the 'Trying Twenties'. At this stage the young adult may seek to build a clear structure for his or her future. Unless this is accompanied by self-examination, this may result in premature rigidity—a position of being locked into a given identity. Alternatively the twenties may be a period of exploration and experiment. Towards the end of the decade comes the 'Catch-30' crisis. The provisional adult identity of the twenties may be experienced as restrictive, and the turn of the decade may be marked by new choices and a new vitality. The early thirties are a period of 'Rooting and Extending'. Life becomes less provisional, and the person may settle down. Age 35–45 is the 'Deadline Decade'—the halfway mark of life and an inner crossroads. This is the period for a mid-life crisis to develop. After the mid-forties or so, it is possible for equilibrium to be regained, as the adult enters a period of 'Renewal or Resignation'.

6.14 The indications are that life after adolescence is in no sense one long plateau, but is marked by continuing growth and development. Lack of personal awareness of the inevitability of such changes leaves one unprepared and ill-equipped to handle development crises constructively, and may result in unnecessary stagnation. There is an increasing awareness, in secular and religious literature, of adult development crises, and it is important that such thought should be adequately taken into the general understanding of Christian initiation and growth.

6.15 The late teens and early twenties are only the beginning of adulthood, and are marked by a provisional adult identity. The Confirmation of a young adult is the Confirmation of someone in this provisional stage of entry to adult life. He or she has in no real sense 'arrived', but will undergo further developmental crises. If Confirmation is seen, as it often is, as the end of a process, this will conflict with its developmental significance. Thus, the Confirmation of a young adult may become a self-contradictory and confusing act, on a developmental perspective. It takes place at the time of the initial adult developmental crisis, and should therefore look forward to further development. Yet, by confirming in late adolescence, we provide ritual support and help in the first adult developmental crisis only. In fact, we often pre-empt the matter by confirming in early adolescence, and so offer no ritual support in any adult developmental crisis.

6.16 While the primary focus of our report is on the admission of persons (usually of young age) to Communion before Confirmation, the wider issues of continuing nurture and personal development in the faith may not be ignored.

6.17 Many churches have introduced opportunities for all ages to learn together, and from one another. Community education programmes are being developed in secular educational institutions, but in parish situations they are in their infancy. A more 'successful' approach has been to recognise the importance of worship as a 'learning experience'. There has been debate about the nature of worship and the appropriateness of combining teaching and worship (or, for that matter, teaching and preaching). That is to miss the point. Our concern must be with what is *learned* on such occasions—not with what is taught. Within the context of worship, children and adults have begun to share their faith with each other and to learn from each other.

6.18 None of these points is to suggest that structured programmes are unimportant. Neither do they underestimate the contribution of the support of a Christian home. Indeed what has been said about children and adults learning together applies very much to the relationship between a child and parent(s).

6.19 Peer group meetings and their 'teaching schemes' complement the other broader experiences outlined above. For children, this means providing a time for reflection on 'what happens in church'; helping them to look at patterns that they have discovered in worship and pointing them to other important features. The peer group is the place where they can share their own ideas much more freely. They will also be given information; some of the 'why?' how?' questions—important to primary school age children—will be asked and answered in a way appropriate to their understanding. Here too will be an introduction to biblical material and Bible stories. Even at a young age children experience 'the dark side of life' and these informal groups, supported by sensitive adults, may begin to explore some of the ideas of death, loss, broken relationships. All these features may contribute to a growing 'spirituality' for the child, so that faith and life become fused.

6.20 We do not deny the value of the intellect, but question any over-emphasis on intellectual capability in the Christian life. We are saved by grace through faith, not by intellect, and it is therefore unfortunate that the two are often treated as synonymous, by interpreting faith as the intellectual grasp of doctrinal teaching. We do not wish to devalue the teaching of Christian doctrine at any stage of life, but see it taking its place within a scale of priorities in Christian education. There is a tremendous need for teaching on prayer and on growth in the Christian life. The latter is particularly important in connection with adult development crises. The Christian response to these must rightly include a balanced doctrine of providence and a practical understanding of how to wait on God to seek his will and guidance in all the situations of life.

6.21 The alternative practice of admitting children to Communion prior to Confirmation has developed in some parishes as a result of taking seriously the preparation necessary for Confirmation. In these and other parishes there has been an emphasis on 'education' understood in terms of Christian nurture as outlined above. This form of parish education has rarely been seen simply in terms of 'training' or 'instruction' in preparation for an 'adult mode-of-being' in the Christian community. From the theological perspective it has been held that the admission to Communion is a means of grace by which the recipient is helped to grow towards greater maturity. It should be recognised that the act of receiving Communion, and indeed the awareness of the right to receive, is itself also a major tool of Christian education. It teaches not only the child but also the adult. It proclaims in a concrete way that belonging to Christ's body is a gift of grace. In this sense, the action says more simply what sermons also seek to convey. If an alternative practice is implemented for the future, it requires the Church to develop its educational policies and practices for Christians at all ages and stages of faith.

---

[1] Reported in *The Month,* October 1984.

[2] British Council of Churches, *Understanding Christian Nurture,* para. 63.

[3] *Ibid;* para. 58.

[4] *Ibid;* para. 65.

[5] J.W. Fowler, *Stages of Faith* (1981), J.H. Westerhoff III, *Will our Children have faith?* (1976), Westerhoff & Willimon, *Liturgy and Learning Through the Life Cycle* (1980), G. Moran, *Religious Education Development* (1983).

[6] British Council of Churches, *The Child in the Church,* p. 18.

CHAPTER 7

The Impetus for Change

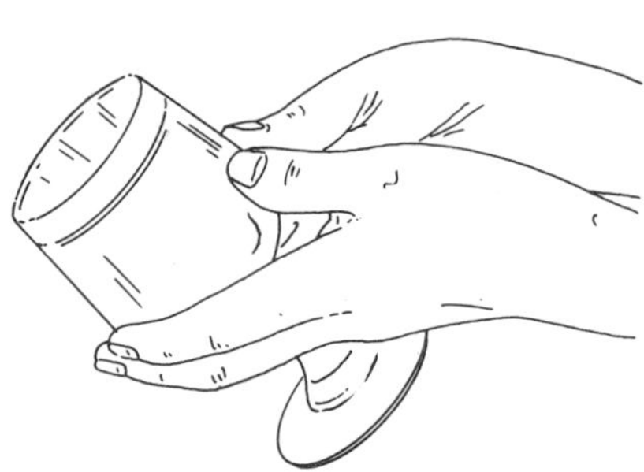

7.1 The twentieth century has seen a variety of approaches to our understanding of Initiation and there has been a succession of reports. There have also been changes in parish Sunday practice which underlie most of the synodical debating of the last decade and a half. The arrival of the 'Parish Communion' has had the most far-reaching implications for family involvement in the Eucharist. The starting point of this development is usually traced to December 1927, when St John's, Newcastle-upon-Tyne, started its '9.15', inaugurating a pattern of worship which grew slowly during the 1930s. In the post-war years, it expanded rapidly. Children were now present in church every week, with their parents, at the main Eucharist during which their parents would receive Communion. It was also at St John's that there began, in the late 1930s, the blessing of the unconfirmed at the altar rail, and the whole pattern which we still experience came into use. Children went up to the rail and shared, as fully as the discipline would allow, in their parents' Communion. The process started to set up desires, in both parents and children, for children to be allowed to communicate. These desires were sometimes met by a downwards shift in the age of Confirmation and sometimes by a justification of the existing discipline and practice.

Insoluble tensions were set up which produced an impetus for change.

7.2 The Ely Report, when it reviewed the whole question of Christian Initiation (1971), suggested three reasons for change in the present practice. These were:

> The theological and linguistic confusion over the whole theology and practice of Christian Initiation, which has made it necessary to give detailed consideration to Baptism as well as Confirmation;
>
> The continual decline in the number of candidates for Confirmation, particularly noticeable among boys, and the continued lapsing after Confirmation;
>
> The fact that the Church has failed to grasp the opportunity of training children and young people for Christian life in the world at one of the main points of contact in its educational ministry with the young.

7.2.1 The report concluded with sixteen specific recommendations. Ten of these were concerned with Pastoral practice or liturgical provision.[1] Of the remaining six, four concerned Confirmation and the reception of non-Anglicans into the Church of England, and are not part of this discussion. The remaining two are:

> 154.1 The Church should make explicit its recognition of Baptism as the full and complete rite of Christian Initiation.
>
> 157.1 It should be permissible for the Parish Priest, at his discretion, to admit persons to Communion (if they so desire) who have been baptised with water in the name of the Trinity.[2]

7.2.2 The essential question that underlies these recommendations is *'what more than Baptism is needed?'*. It is a fact that the one rite of initiation has become divided into two parts; what is not clear is whether (a) both parts are necessary, or (b) one part will 'do', or (c) that one part is actually sufficient. What is clear is that in the case of (b) and (c) the part must be Baptism. The report *Confirmation Today* (1944) stated that the distinction between 'membership' and 'full membership' is meaningless and unknown in the New Testament. The Ely Report's recommendations, had they been accepted, would have given substance to that statement. In the event the response of the dioceses to the Ely Report was confusing and, although General Synod had recommended 157.1 initially to the dioceses, when it came back to Synod the way ahead was not clear.

7.2.3 Since 1976 there have been a number of important developments, within the Church of England, elsewhere in the Anglican Communion, and also in other Churches.[3] *The Alternative Service Book* and the Lima Document on *Baptism, Eucharist and Ministry* have been published and have their influence on the debate.

7.3 THE ALTERNATIVE SERVICE BOOK

7.3.1 The anomalies of the present situation become more clear when Infant Baptism is administered in the context of the Eucharist. In para. 58 (p. 248) of the *Alternative Service Book* (ASB), the newly baptised baby is welcomed into the Christian community:

Priest: God has received you by Baptism into his Church.

All: We welcome you into the Lord's family.
We are members together of the body of Christ;
We are children of the same heavenly Father;
We are inheritors together of the kingdom of God.
We welcome you.

We are instructed (p. 250) that 'The service then follows the Holy Communion service from the Peace (section 30)'. This reads (p. 128) either 'Christ is our peace . . . . .' or 'We are the Body of Christ . . . . .' (and there are alternatives in section 83 (p. 170). At section 43 (p. 42) there is said:

President: We break this Bread to share in the Body of Christ.

All Though we are many, we are one body,
because we all share in one bread.

The invitation to Communion (section 45) and the words for the distribution (section 46) remind us of our participation in the Body of Christ *except,* that is, the newly baptised infant whom we have welcomed into the Body with one hand and then shunned with the other.

7.3.2 Valiant attempts have been made to include children in the action of worship: they have been welcomed to the altar rail. But instead of receiving there the sign of belonging, they receive a gesture which, in an adult setting, reinforces the impression of their unacceptability. The more emphasis is placed on 'commitment' in Baptism, the clearer stands out the non-commitment of the Church towards the baptised. Such a withholding of our commitment cannot be reconciled with the Christian teaching about a 'God who first loved us'.

7.3.3 Two texts are important. First, I Cor. 10. 16b–17 (JB) which reads '. . . . . the bread that we break is a communion with the Body of

Christ. The fact that there is only one loaf means that, though there are many of us, we form a single body because we all have a share in this one loaf.' Also I Cor. 11. 28, 29 (JB) which reads: 'Everyone is to recollect himself before eating the bread and drinking this cup; because a person who eats and drinks without recognising the Body is eating and drinking his own condemnation.' There seems to be demanded some awareness of both the corporate nature of the Church and the significance of the Eucharist itself before admission to Communion.

7.3.4 The awareness that is expected, however, is according to the capacity of the person involved. Many Orthodox Christians are happy to understand what is required as 'an awareness of being loved', and such a requirement is capable of including the very young, and very old, and the mentally handicapped. There is no denying that even comparatively young children can have a very real awareness of the 'specialness' of the Communion within the Eucharist just as there is no denying that the seemingly senile *still* express a desire to receive their Communion, which is readily given.

7.3.5 Significantly, the ASB is here expressing a change in the Church's own awareness of itself, pointing towards a model of the church that speaks much more strongly of human loving being a mirror of the divine love. Just as children receive the totality of human loving so they are entitled to receive the totality of God's grace.

7.4 BAPTISM, EUCHARIST AND MINISTRY—THE LIMA REPORT

7.4.1 The debate on this document is only in its earliest stages, but one of the points with which the Church of England will have to come to terms occurs in the commentary on para. 14:

> If baptism, as incorporation into the body of Christ, points by its very nature to the eucharist sharing of Christ's body and blood, the question arises as to how a further and separate rite can be interposed between baptism and admission to communion. Those churches which baptise children but refuse them a share in the eucharist before such a rite may wish to ponder whether they have fully appreciated and accepted the consequences of baptism.[4]

7.4.2 Lewis Mudge points out: 'The document deals skilfully with the differences of baptismal practice in Protestantism. The fact that the differences are of "practice", and no longer of "faith", is the heart of the matter'.[5] He then goes on to explore the problems of a sacramental interpretation of Confirmation before developing the idea that the reason why there is now convergence on Baptism is that it is becoming the fundamental sacrament of unity prior to and transcending ecclesiastical divisions.[6]

7.4.3 Underlying these converging ideas is the firm reassertion that Christian Initiation is 'Grace received' and not 'achievement recorded'.

7.5 THE CURRENT STATE OF CONFIRMATION

7.5.1 There is theological uncertainty about the nature of the gift or grace conferred by Confirmation, and a greater willingness to see it as of less significance than was thought previously. One indication is the readiness to admit Free Church communicants; the strength of the desire to admit young children to Communion before Confirmation is another. Confirmation is less and less seen as a necessary sacramental component of Christian initiation.

7.5.2 However, there are three clearly definable elements in Anglican Confirmation as received from earlier generations. They are:

(a) Confirmation as admission to Communion.

(b) Confirmation as ratification by an adult believer of baptismal vows made by proxy in infancy.

(c) Confirmation as the reception of the 'confirming' grace of the Holy Spirit.

These first two elements are contrary the one to the other in terms of the *age* for Confirmation: (a) is always trying to push the age down, as the desire to admit children to Communion bears upon it; (b) is always trying to push the age up, as the expectation that the candidate will be an adult believer requires an older age than early teens to be credible.

7.5.3 Thus, the commonly found age of Confirmation in the Church of England, about 12 years, can be seen as an uneasy compromise between the conflicting principles, with the age veering up or down according to the relative force of these two principles in any particular parish. The difficulties in instructing, in incorporating, and perhaps in keeping, candidates on the current age basis is an indication that we are confirming most people at an age when we are least likely to be effective in enabling understanding or encouraging commitment.

7.5.4 Confirmation is a boundary which Anglicans currently have to cross before they can receive Communion. This has sometimes led to the creation of a 'second-class' Anglican, baptised but not confirmed, especially in young adult communities such as chaplaincy groups in Higher Education. The situation is now aggravated by the passing of Canon B15A, which permits all those 'in good standing with their own church' to receive Communion at an Anglican Eucharist. Although the Canon goes on to say that people who regularly attend Anglican churches should be made aware of 'normal requirements', they are allowed to receive the sustenance of the Eucharist whilst coming to their decision even though they may 'only' have been baptised.

7.5.5 When Confirmation is required as a prerequisite for admission to Communion, it can assume the character of a 'leaving' certificate. This tends to imply that there is no need for further training and an individual's understanding of the Christian faith may remain fixed at that level. A more flexible approach, not requiring people to be confirmed before admission to Communion, could enable the development of more broadly based parish education programmes, for people of all ages.

7.5.6 Lurking behind the array of criticisms is the uncomfortable demand that initiation procedures are supposed to witness for God, and not against his ways. Accordingly, we have to consider the effect on adults as well as children. 'Adultism' (the doctrine that only adults 'really' belong, because they alone have 'achieved' their status) is a distortion of the gospel, which is planted and reinforced for adults, by initiation policies which exalt human initiative over the priority of grace. Adults at the communion rail are encouraged to distinguish themselves from the majority of the baptised (who do not go to church) on the basis of their commitment. They carried through to Confirmation; they bother to get up for church; in short, they see the Church constituted by the convictions and initiative of people like themselves.

7.6 DEVELOPMENTS IN THE CHURCH OF ENGLAND

7.6.1 Ever since the beginning of the Church there has been debate as to who may join and how they should join. The length of the debate shows that it is almost inconceivable that these questions will be simply and comprehensively answered in a way that is acceptable to all. The motion presented to General Synod on behalf of Winchester Diocese in 1981 gave expression to an unease with the present position in the Church of England.

7.6.2 The pressure for review, and possible change, of the relationship between Confirmation and admission to Communion is reflected in the number of diocesan working parties which have been asked to report on the question. (To date, 14 dioceses are known to have initiated such working parties.)

7.6.3 Despite the fact that the Church of England has affirmed no change in its rules, nevertheless some dioceses have given recognition to the practice in parishes of admitting to Communion before Confirmation. Other dioceses have experienced pressure for such a change, but have felt constrained by the rules.

7.6.4 We have sought information from diocesan bishops as to the basis upon which permission has been given and contacted a selected number of parishes (twenty) of differing types to learn of their experience in admitting children and young people to Communion. In some dioceses the permitting of an alternative practice has been introduced only recently and little information is available, as yet. Others have a longer history of admitting to Communion and have supplied us with information as to how parishes have operated the policy over a span of up to ten years. No complete statistics exist to record the extent of the development in the Church of England and we have not attempted to do more than detail the current position with regard to diocesan policies and, out of the information received from parishes, list some of the principles which appear to be significant.

7.6.5 (a) Dioceses with a declared policy of permitting admission to Communion before Confirmation.	—	4
(b) Dioceses granting specific permission to individual parishes for a period.	—	19

No account is taken here of dioceses in which parishes may be acting unofficially in admitting to Communion.

7.6.6 There are also some dioceses which have recognised a pressure for permission to be given, but where a decision has been deferred pending a further discussion in General Synod.

7.6.7 A number of bishops and parish clergy have, most helpfully, supplied details of their practice of admitting children to Communion before Confirmation. There appear, broadly speaking, to be two approaches:

(a) where admission to Communion is seen as part of a specific programme of preparation for Confirmation in the future;

(b) where persons are admitted to Communion, with or without a minimum age stipulated, with Confirmation being seen as a separate event at a much later stage.

Inevitably, there is much variety in practice, both in terms of the age of entry and in the treatment of those who decide not to proceed to Confirmation. Two case studies, reflecting the principles and practice of these two main approaches, blending information received from parishes, are included at the end of this chapter.

7.6.8 Despite the variety in practice, it is possible to highlight the following principles and discoveries about such practice:

(a) The need to prepare for the introduction of an alternative practice by wide discussion and agreement within the parish.

(b) The importance of individual pastoral care, in the case of each child, or adult, in making the decision to admit to Communion at any particular time, and to keep a register of those so admitted.

(c) The need to consider carefully the public profile given to the actual reception of First Communion.

(d) The need to provide adequate adult support, whether through communicant parents or other suitable adult sponsors.

(e) The need to have an adequate system of referral to a new parish when families move, with direct contact between the incumbents concerned.

Few problems have been encountered in moving to a different parish; in some cases it has been possible for communicant children to continue to receive Communion, in others an earlier than customary presentation for Confirmation has been appropriate. The experience of parishes consulted is that the pastoral care of such families, when they move, is handled positively and has enabled them to be easily welcomed into their new parish. A 'mixed pattern' has existed for some time in parishes receiving Anglicans from Canada and the USA into their congregations.

(f) The introduction of such a practice challenges the congregation to become a more effective and responsible nurturing community. It is sometimes found difficult to persuade sufficient members of the congregation to take on specific responsibilities for work with children, particularly where there are extended periods of specific pre-Confirmation preparation.

(g) The difficulty is met, on occasion, of convincing parents and others that baptised children are already members of the body of Christ, and that admission to first Communion is not an alternative form of Confirmation.

7.6.9 The experience of those who have introduced the practice of admitting to Communion after Baptism and before Confirmation indicates that it raises questions about baptismal policy and the meaning of membership. Additional demands are made on a parish's resources for pastoral care, and it is not yet clear whether those so admitted will continue as practising communicants. Parishes who have introduced such a practice, however, have done so on the basis of what had been felt to be theologically and pastorally appropriate rather than for practical expediency. It is often in parishes where the pattern of worship includes a 'Family Eucharist' that the need to admit children to Communion is most strongly felt.

7.6.10 PARISH CASE STUDIES

In detailing these two differing parish approaches, we have merged the information supplied by questionnaire returns from parishes to present composite pictures.

Parish Type A—admission to Communion as part of specific Confirmation preparation.

This practice has been long established (ten years or so) and the permission of the bishop was sought at its inception. Discussions took place in the PCC, with the congregation in general and with neighbouring clergy before the practice was introduced. Baptised children who have been regular church attenders, and/or have been members of the Sunday School, are invited, with the consent of their parents, to join the junior membership group at around the age of 11/12, though in some cases a year or so younger. During a period of preparation for admission to Communion, lasting about two or three months, the children receive instruction about the significance of sharing the sacrament of Holy Communion, with adults from the congregation taking part along with the clergy. At the end of the period of instruction, the children are admitted to Communion, not at a special service, but, with special mention made of the fact, at the Sunday Eucharist. Their names are recorded in a special register and each receives a copy of the *Alternative Service Book*. During the next three years they continue to meet as a junior membership group for a programme of instruction and social activities leading to Confirmation. It is pointed out at the start of the process that leaving the group means that they must cease to be communicants until they are confirmed.

Parish Type B—admission to Communion other than as part of a specific pre-Confirmation group.

In this parish, the practice has been more recently introduced (two years ago) and, again, full consultation at many levels took place prior to its inception. A minimum age of seven years has been set for the admission of baptised children to Communion, but it has sometimes been found necessary to defer such an admission, or to allow younger children to be admitted. Children are admitted on the decision of the incumbent, at the request of, and after discussion with, the children themselves, their parents or other adults in the congregation. There is usually simple preparation before Communion is first received, quite informal and individually given. No form of admission service is used and there is no particular Sunday during the year when children are admitted to Communion. The congregation is asked to pray especially for such children at the Eucharist when they will first receive Communion. The children and their parents are told that, because they are fully members of the church through their Baptism and so able to receive Communion, it is anticipated that they will want to equip themselves for adult Christian life by taking part in the parish's educational programmes, and, at an appropriate point, make an adult commitment in Confirmation. The parish has adopted a policy of not presenting anyone for Confirmation before the age of sixteen. No penalty attaches to those who, although communicants, do not come forward for Confirmation, though every opportunity will be taken to challenge and encourage them to make a public commitment to Christ by being confirmed.

[1] *Christian Initiation: The Ely Report* GS 30 (1970), pp. 48, 49.
[2] *Ibid,* p. 48.
[3] See Appendix 2.
[4] *Baptism, Eucharist and Ministry,* Faith and Order Paper No. 111, (1982), p. 5.
[5] L. Mudge, *Ecumenical Perspectives on Baptism, Eucharist and Ministry,* p. 37.
[6] *Ibid,* pp. 42, 43.

CHAPTER 8

A Way Forward and some Implications

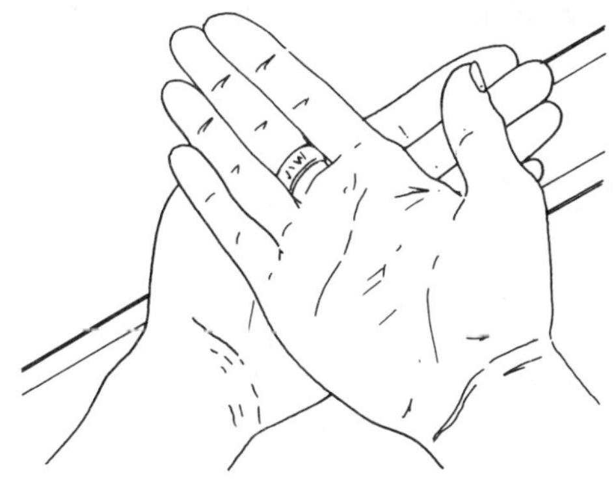

8.1 The question of membership and of entry into membership is confused in the Church of England. Sectarian groups are able to operate a strictly controlled membership policy and to manage clearly the boundary between the church and the world. For the Church of England, the historic interweaving of Church and society has created expectations that a broadly-based public ministry will be offered. Such expectations must be recognised, whether or not they are welcomed, and contribute to the difficulty of rigidly determining our membership boundaries. Such is the backcloth against which the present debate about Christian initiation and admission to Communion is conducted.

8.2 We have tried, in tracing the history of our present tradition, to clarify in it that which is of doctrine and that which is of discipline, and so to cut through some of the theological confusion surrounding Christian Initiation. We have recognised that the significantly changed, and changing, nature of society makes redundant many of the assumptions underlying our current practice.

8.3 From our theological review, we are assured that the Church of England has rightly asserted that Baptism is the sacrament by which a person becomes a full member of the Church. The implied corollary to this is that admission to Communion needs no further sacramental validation. The voiced requests of children and parents to permit a full sharing in eucharistic fellowship by those baptised into full membership cannot be ignored without danger of ignoring the gospel of grace. Educational and sociological considerations suggest that, as a question quite distinct from that of admission to Communion, the early teens are a most inappropriate time to encourage or require a 'once-for-all' public faith commitment of the kind that we deem Confirmation to be.

8.4 We have indicated how an impetus for a change in practice by permitting the admission of baptised persons to Communion before Confirmation has begun to develop in the Church of England and in other Churches. It seems to us desirable to advocate such a change, not because it will immediately solve all the confusion about Church of England membership, but because it would be theologically and pastorally appropriate. Such a move, to permit change, without requiring it, could enable dioceses and parishes to proceed at a pace that would be determined by pastoral need and able to be pastorally supportable. New questions would be raised by the adoption of such a policy and we explore below some of the implications.

8.5 IMPLICATIONS OF A CHANGE IN PRACTICE

8.5.1 *Implications for Confirmation*

If unconfirmed children are admitted to Communion, then certain results follow for Confirmation:

(a) Confirmation can no longer be expounded to be absolutely necessary to Christian Initiation—a corollary of asserting that Baptism is sufficient. It would, therefore, become a rite which episcopal Churches retain and use, although not indispensable to the making of a Christian.

(b) Confirmation would cease necessarily to imply or to convey admission to Communion.

(c) Certain other elements which feature in Anglican Confirmation would remain and continue to have significance:

the opportunity for an adult ratification of baptismal vows;

the sacramental opportunity to focus the continuing gift of God's Grace;

the linking of individual faith and the local congregation to the whole church through the presence of the bishop.

(d) Confirmation would, in all probability, be sought at an older age than that which is currently common, determined by a variety of factors affecting when individuals might be recognised as having adult status. The current age of admission to the Electoral Roll is 16 and it is possible that Confirmation might be regarded as being linked with enfranchisement for exercising responsibility in the church.

8.5.2 *Implications for parishes, during a period of transition*

(a) *Decision-taking:* parishes wishing to change will need to make a clear decision at some point that i) they will admit children to Communion under the conditions which may be defined by Synod, and ii) they will begin a new discipline of Confirmation. Such a decision will need very thorough preparation and a very high level of support. It may be easier if there is a prior diocesan decision or recommendation, but, in general, it will be a parish decision which is determinative.

(b) *A new pattern:* it may be that the age of Confirmation may in principle rise from, say, 11–12 to 15–17. If this happens all at once, then there will be families where one child was confirmed last year, and the next one expects to be next year—and suddenly it has been indefinitely postponed, or so it seems. This may well be more of a problem to 'fringe' people than within committed families (where the children will be communicant and within the parish system).

(c) *Parishes which decide not to change:* there may be various reasons, theological or non-theological, which will bring a parish to decide not to proceed with the changed pattern. The 'transitional' problems which will arise for them will be through the arrival in the parish of young children who are already communicants, enrolled and registered as such. These, if numerous, could prove an embarrassment to a parish's existing pattern, and to that extent parishes which do change will slowly come to exert pressure on those which do not.

(d) We believe that the first admission to Communion of a child should not be seen as an alternative Confirmation. We recommend parishes to adopt a low-profile approach, with children being admitted informally and individually at no particular age. Mention could be made at the beginning of the Eucharist, and the children could be prayed for by name, when they are first to receive Communion. This would help to guard against the excesses from which Confirmation sometimes suffers as a social event.

8.5.3 Godparents have a liturgical role in Baptism, and are normally invited to be present at their godchild's Confirmation, which marks the end of their official duties. It would be valuable for them to be involved in the child's first Communion. Admission of children to Communion before Confirmation would enhance the role of godparents, along with parents and the church congregation, in supporting the young person through the traumas of adolescence and early adulthood. It is, of course, not only in the spiritual lives of the young that mentors have a part to play: spiritual counsellors and Christian friends, either singly or in house or prayer groups, can give much needed support and encouragement at times of stress or crisis.

8.5.4 If dioceses were to make a rapid and thorough change to the new pattern, bishops could soon find that, for an interim period, only a few teenage candidates were presented for Confirmation, and the total number of candidates could, at least for a while, show a marked decline. However, no bishop considers his pastoral ministry exclusively restricted to, or defined by, his conduct of Confirmations. Moreover, both bishops and parish priests will need to urge adult people to seek Confirmation, for it will still be an occasion of importance when believing Christians make a personal profession of faith and express a desire, purposefully, to lead a life of worship and witness within the fellowship of our communion. After the profession of faith, the imposition of the bishop's hand will continue to assure the candidates and the congregation that God supplies spiritual gifts to enable the candidates to persevere in the life-long commitment which is implicit in a mature profession of faith.

CHAPTER 9

Conclusions and Recommendations

9.1 From our review of the origins and meaning of Confirmation as practised in the Church of England we conclude:

(a) that Baptism with water, in the name of the Holy Trinity, is a complete sacrament of Initiation into the Body of Christ;

(b) that Confirmation is not an absolutely necessary prerequisite for the admission of persons to Holy Communion;

(c) that it is desirable, both for clarity of principle and for effective pastoral practice, to permit the admission of baptised persons to Holy Communion, before Confirmation;

(d) that Confirmation should remain in the Church of England as a sacramental means of grace to accompany an adult profession of faith.

9.2 We recommend:

(a) that a regulation along the lines of the draft appended to this chapter be approved by the General Synod of the Church of England;

(b) that the Standing Committee be requested to ensure that parishes are assisted to discuss, formulate and implement an appropriate policy and to develop effective educational strategies for Christian growth.

9.3 DRAFT REGULATION (MADE PURSUANT TO CANON B15A, PARAGRAPH 1C)
Admission of Baptised Persons to Holy Communion before Confirmation
A Baptised children who have not yet come to 'years of discretion' and thus are not eligible for Confirmation (Canon B27, paragraph 3) may be admitted to Holy Communion under the following conditions:

(i) that the Bishop of the Diocese has been consulted.

(ii) that the incumbent and the PCC of the parish have recommended to a meeting of those on the Electoral Roll specially convened for that purpose, and that meeting has accepted by a two-thirds majority of those present and voting, that the parish and its ministers could admit children to Communion under the provisions of this regulation.

(iii) that the incumbent is satisfied that Christian education appropriate to the age of the children concerned is being provided for them.

(iv) that the incumbent enters the names of the children who are to be admitted to Communion in a Register kept for that purpose.

(v) that when such children come to years of discretion, and after due instruction as required by Canon B27, the incumbent shall present them to the Bishop for Confirmation.

B The Diocesan Synod may, but need not, pass a resolution concerning a minimum age for admission to Communion under paragraph A above.

C The PCC may by resolution provide for a minimum age in the parish which may be different from that contained in any resolution of the Diocesan Synod.

D A child whose name has been entered into a Parish Register under paragraph A(iv) above, shall be given a Certificate of his Communicant status in the Church of England and no such Communicant child may be excluded from Communion in any other parish of the Church of England, notwithstanding the fact that this age may be lower than the minimum age permitted by that diocese or parish.

E A decision to admit children to Communion under paragraph A(ii) above, shall be reversed only by a two-thirds majority of those present and voting at an Annual Parochial Church Meeting of the parish.

NOTES ON THE ABOVE DRAFT REGULATION

The regulation is drafted to provide both clear boundaries and local flexibility. It does not of itself touch on any national minimum age, the manner of admission to Communion, or any standard of achievement in understanding or discipleship.

There might perhaps be a requirement (whether by regulation or administrative action) that dioceses should keep a central record of parish decisions, and that the General Synod office should compile annually a register of diocesan positions.

APPENDICES

Appendix 1 Guidelines for parishes concerning the admission of children to Holy Communion

The Regulation approved by General Synod provides a framework for the admission of baptised persons to Holy Communion before Confirmation on the basis of their Baptism alone, as far as sacramental initiation is concerned. These informal guidelines are provided for the assistance of parishes wishing to implement the policy permitted by the Regulations.

(i) No change should take place without a parish taking the following steps. Its incumbent and PCC should debate the issues concerned and should reach a clear decision. It would be wise for a PCC to stipulate a two-thirds majority as a basis for its recommendation of a change in policy to the special Church Meeting convened for this purpose. Notice of the motion coming before the Church Meeting should be given in the usual way, and the motion should take the form:

> 'This Church Meeting, duly convened, resolves to admit children to Communion under the provisions of Canon B15A 1(c) and the Regulation made thereunder.'

(ii) A PCC *may* provide for a minimum age, and give other guidance to ministers and parents.

(iii) Parents or other adults who bring children to Communion should produce evidence of their children's Baptism.

(iv) The parish priest shall register the names of those admitted to Communion.

(v) The incumbent and PCC should assume responsibility for monitoring whether such children continue as communicants, and contact with the supporting adults should be maintained to this end.

(vi) A parish should assume particular responsibility for nurturing new communicants within its framework of Christian education.

(vii) Further detailed provision should be made for:

(a) Receiving and commending children when parents move from one parish to another;

(b) Preparing baptised communicants for Confirmation;

(c) Deciding how young children who express a wish to receive Communion but have not been baptised may best be prepared for Baptism and at what stage of their maturity they may most appropriately be baptised.

(viii) First Communion: the regulation does not provide for any special ceremony in relation to admitting the baptised to Communion. Rather, it should be wholly natural for worshipping children to become communicants without any special ceremony, at whatever time they are ready. Whilst registration is necessary, questioning, during the Eucharist, of those being admitted or the provision of a formal admission, is undesirable. Mention of the person in the prayers and possibly a welcome expressed in the notices or at the kiss of peace is sufficient. If it is considered appropriate for the bishop himself to take part in any ceremony, care will need to be taken to avoid any impression that it is Confirmation that is being administered.

Appendix 2 Developments in Other Churches

In the light of all that has been said about the changed context of Christian faith in our day, it is not surprising to discover that the Church of England is not alone in reviewing the issues of Baptism and admission to Communion. We present here a resumé of the information received from other parts of the Church.

THE ANGLICAN COMMUNION

Churches within the Anglican Communion can be grouped into three categories over this issue:

(a) those which have changed their policy;
(b) those which are considering change;
(c) those which have not yet changed.

(a) *Churches which have changed*

New Zealand: after ten years of official experiment, the 1980 General Synod regularised the approval of alternative practice and issued comprehensive guidelines.

United States of America: the 1979 Book of Common Prayer provisions can be interpreted in either an Eastern or Western way. The service of Baptism includes elements which some regard as Confirmation, whereas others interpret the Form of Commitment to Christian Service as capable of being understood as Confirmation. Either view, however, provides grounds for communicating infants and young children and the evidence for this is widespread and increasing.

Canada: dioceses are free to make their own decision on the question and almost all admit children from the age of five years onwards.

South Africa: after acknowledgement by Synod (1980) of Baptism as the complete sacramental rite of initiation, approval was given for a period of experiment. Diocesan bishops may authorise the admission of young children to Communion, in their local congregation only.

The Scottish Episcopal Church: the Synod decided in 1978 to permit the admission of children to Communion before Confirmation.

(b) *Churches which are considering change*
Australia: In 1981 a provisional Canon was passed by General Synod to permit children to receive Communion before Confirmation, but this did not receive sufficient approval from diocesan synods. A major survey in 1984 has shown that a considerable number of dioceses are, in fact, encouraging the new pattern. It is likely that the 1985 General Synod will be asked to approve a further provisional Canon.

England

(c) *Churches which have not yet changed*
Ireland: no developments, other than a exploratory paper to the Board of Education.

Wales: a questionnaire has been circulated to all parishes and a report may be produced.

Central Africa: the Confirmation age is around eighteen years. Only a minority of dioceses follow an Episcopal Synod ruling (mid 1970s) that a bishop can admit children before Confirmation.

Zaire, the Southern Cone of South America, Uganda, Kenya, Burma, West Africa, Papua New Guinea, and Hong Kong report no change.

THE ORTHODOX CHURCH

The normal practice of the Orthodox Churches is to offer full Christian Initiation to young infants, at which they become full communicants in their own right. There is no question of admission to Communion without Chrismation, the Orthodox equivalent of Confirmation.

Full initiation involves exorcism, Baptism and Chrismation, all following immediately after each other in one service. Chrismation involves anointing the candidate a number of times, and at each anointing the priest says: 'The seal of the gift of the Holy Spirit'. There is no laying-on-of-hands, and the normal minister of this sacrament is a priest. The presence of a bishop is not required but his prior blessing of the oils is essential. Chrismation is not understood as the renewal of Baptism, but as lay Ordination. In later years the child may learn to prepare for Communion with fasting, and with confession. (There is no fixed age for this, but eight is a possible age.)

Communion is received in both kinds, together, as a morsel of bread soaked in wine. This is true for both adults and children, but it is necessary to mention this in the case of children, since otherwise one might struggle to visualise a babe-in-arms attempting to cope with a wafer and a chalice!

The great strength of Orthodox practice is the fact that children grow up with a full involvement in this central sacrament. They have never been excluded and it is something normal and natural for them, a formative influence right from the very start. A possible weakness of Orthodox practice is the fact that there is no later sacrament or ceremony by which adolescent or adult commitment may be affirmed. There is no adult 'rite of passage', no specific provision for linking any or all of the stages of adult development with religious commitment.

THE ROMAN CATHOLIC CHURCH (IN ENGLAND)

The picture is one of both clarity and flux. The emphasis is on Baptism as complete sacrament of Initiation. Admission to Communion follows, at the discretion of the parish priest, after first confession, sometime during childhood. Confirmation does not take place before the age of seven and there are differing opinions as to what is an appropriate age. The Bishops' Conference received a proposal to raise the minimum age for Confirmation (Easter 1985) and agreed to allow each diocese to determine its own policy on the question.

THE METHODIST CHURCH

In 1984 the Division of Education and Youth reported to the Methodist Conference as follows:

> There is wide divergence in practice amongst us with regard to children and Holy Communion. In some churches they are not normally present at all; in others they are passively present in their seats; in others they come to the Holy Table with parents or leaders to receive a blessing; in yet others they receive the bread and wine. This diversity is confusing and unsatisfactory to the extent that society is increasingly mobile, and perhaps two or three times in their early life children may move to churches with quite widely variant practices. The Division believes the time has now come for the Methodist Church to adopt as its policy the encouragement of fuller participation by children in

> Holy Communion and urges on all churches, very strongly, the vital need to adopt no practice that appears to the child to deny the baptismal promises or to nullify the growing child's own 'human response'.

The Conference approved the report and directed the Division to consult with the Faith and Order Committee and to bring to Conference, not later than 1986, proposals to encourage the fuller participation of children in the sacrament of Holy Communion.

THE CHURCH OF SCOTLAND

In 1982 the General Assembly of the Church of Scotland adopted proposals from the Church's Education Department which would permit baptised children to receive the sacrament of Holy Communion. Under the terms of the Barrier Act, the matter was referred to local presbyteries for a subsequent Assembly to convert the recommendations into Standing Law. Insufficient support was given to the proposal by presbyteries and the Assembly, accordingly, has not made a decision to proceed.

THE UNITED REFORMED CHURCH

Current practice varies greatly between congregations: in some, children are required to leave halfway through the Eucharist; in others children are welcomed as communicants. A common practice is to allow the reception of Communion by the baptised children of parents who are church members, either regularly or on special occasions after specific preparation. Where children receive Communion, six to seven years is the usual age for this to begin. The Doctrine and Worship Committee have not yet made any statement on the question, although a Working Party (jointly with the Children's Work Committee) has now been set up.

THE BAPTIST UNION

A consultation on Children and Holy Communion held in 1985 received papers describing the theology and educational factors requiring to be considered. It is unlikely that a central policy will be declared, since local churches may make their own autonomous decisions. The issue is being raised, primarily, in local ecumenical projects and in churches developing a greater emphasis on family worship. It is the practice of the Baptist Church to baptise adults only.

BRITISH COUNCIL OF CHURCHES WORKING PARTY

In 1984 the British Council of Churches set up a Working Party on the Theology and Practice of Christian Initiation and Church Membership. The primary task of the group is to explore ways forward towards an understanding of common church membership.

Appendix 3 'At What Age . . . . .?'

5 years—	full-time education compulsory
	U or PG films unaccompanied
	child fare payable on trains and buses
7 years—	can use National Savings account and some banks
10 years—	can be convicted of criminal offences and 'detained'
12 years—	can buy a pet
13 years—	part-time job (with restrictions)
	Bar-mitzvah for Jewish boys
14 years—	can enter pub, own air rifle, use pawn shop
15 years—	15+ films
	can use Post Office Girobank
16 years—	can leave home without parents' consent
	age of sexual consent for girls
	can marry with parental consent
	can leave school
	permitted to work full-time
	eligible for parish Electoral Roll
	can receive National Insurance number
	can apply for own passport
	can join Trade Union
	can ride moped
	can join Armed Forces (male cadets)
	can buy cigarettes
	can drink beer or wine with a meal in licensed premises
	can buy fireworks
	full fare payable on trains
17 years—	can be sent to prison
	can be licensed to drive most vehicles
	can be elected to Parochial Church Council
	can buy all firearms and ammunition
	can become street trader
	can join Armed Forces (female)
18 years—	become an adult in legal terms
	can vote

	can be elected to deanery, diocesan and General Synods
	can serve on jury
	can buy and drink alcohol in bar
	can join Armed Forces (male adults)
	can be tattooed
	18+ films
19 years—	age at which entitlement to full-time education ceases
21 years—	can become MP or local councillor
	can hold HGV licence
	can apply for licence to sell alcohol

Appendix 4 The Reformation Understanding

A MEMORANDUM PREPARED BY THE REV. MARTIN JACKSON

Baptism

Baptism according to the understanding of the Book of Common Prayer is a rite separate from Confirmation.

Article XXV of the Articles of Religion states:

> There are two Sacraments ordained of Christ our Lord in the Gospel, that is to say, Baptism, and the Supper of the Lord.

As 'sacraments ordained of Christ',

> ..... they be certain sure witnesses, and effectual signs of grace, and God's good will towards us, by the which he doth work invisibly in us, and doth not only quicken, but also strengthen and confirm our Faith in him.

Article XXVII goes on to emphasise the efficacy of Baptism:

> ..... it is a sign of Regeneration or new Birth, whereby, as by an instrument, they that receive Baptism rightly are grafted into the Church; the promises of the forgiveness of sin, and of our adoption to be the sons of God by the Holy Ghost, are visibly signed and sealed: Faith is confirmed, and Grace increased by virtue of prayer unto God .....

While so much is attributed to Baptism, Confirmation receives little mention in the 39 Articles. It is one of the 'five commonly called Sacraments', a group 'as have grown partly of the corrupt following of the Apostles, partly are states of life allowed in the Scriptures'. (Article XXV). The bishops at the Savoy Conference in 1661 defended Confirmation as 'grounded upon the practice of the apostles', citing *Hebrews 6. 2* and *Acts 8. 17*. But the weakness of their case for its necessity may be seen in the conclusion of their response to the Puritan case: 'There is no inconvenience that Confirmation should be required before Communion, when it may be ordinarily obtained'.[1] Confirmation, then, was retained, but its value could be assessed only in terms of what the

Church willed it to have: for it had 'not any visible sign or ceremony ordained of God' and it is the 'sign' of the sacrament which assures us of grace and God's good will towards us—by the sign 'he doth work invisibly in us' (Article XXV). Indeed Cranmer, after denying that scripture gives any indication of the sacramental nature of Confirmation, turns in his answers to the 'Questionnaire' of 1540 to the nature of what is supposed to be the 'sign':

> Of Confirmation with Chrisma, without which it is counted no sacrament, there is no mention in scripture.[2]

His removal of chrismation in the 1549 Confirmation rite, and the removal in 1552 of the consignatory prayer itself indicate that the rite of Confirmation was not to be understood as a sacrament of initiation. It is in Baptism, then, that the individual is grafted into the Church and adopted to be a son of God by the Holy Ghost. It is not necessary to adopt the view that Baptism needs to be supplemented by Confirmation because the inability of infants to declare a personal faith made the initiation less than complete. It is indeed the case that, 'they that receive Baptism *rightly* are grafted into the Church' (Article XXVII), but right reception seems not to relate to the age of the candidate as the final sentence of the Article declares:

> The Baptism of young children is in any wise to be retained in the Church, as most agreeable with the institution of Christ.

Nor can the words of Article XXV be used to argue that a further rite is necessary to bring baptismal grace to full effect:

> ..... in such only as worthily receive the (sacraments) they have a wholesome effect or operation.

For if it were believed that infant Baptism entailed any degree of unworthy reception, then it would necessarily cease to be a practice of the Church:

> ..... that they receive them unworthily purchase to themselves damnation, as Saint Paul saith.

Thus, if an infant may worthily receive Baptism, the sacrament of initiation, we might also ask if consistency does not demand the acknowledgement of its ability to receive the sacrament of Holy Communion. This will be further explored in the next section.

The implications of the Baptismal rite for sacramental participation in the life of the Church

The Prayer Book orders of Public Baptism (of infants) concluded with a direction by the minister of Baptism that the children who have received Baptism should, in due course, be brought for Confirmation. What was directed by rubric in the 1549 and the 1552 rites became in the BCP of 1662 the minister's final words:

> Ye are to take care that this Child be brought to the Bishop to be confirmed by him, so soon as he can say the Creed, the Lord's Prayer, and the Ten Commandments, in the vulgar tongue, and be further instructed in the Church Catechism set forth for that purpose.

Baptism, then, was not all that Church of England discipline required of her members. Indeed, even in the case of those professing their faith for themselves in the 'Public Baptism of such as are of Riper Years', persons recognised as being 'able to answer for themselves' and who would already have been 'sufficiently instructed in the Principles of the Christian Religion',[3] Confirmation was regarded as a pre-condition of admission to Holy Communion. As the first concluding rubric states:

> It is expedient that every person, thus baptized, should be confirmed by the Bishop so soon after his Baptism as conveniently may be; that so he may be admitted to the Holy Communion.

But it could not be said that admission to Holy Communion necessarily depended upon the person coming to Confirmation. This was acknowledged when, as a concession to the Puritans at the Savoy Conference, the rubric concluding the 1662 Order of Confirmation became,

> And there shall none be admitted to this Holy Communion until such time as he be Confirmed, or *be ready and desirous* to be confirmed.

Still there remained the obligation of Confirmation at some stage. Where, however, circumstances had prevented Confirmation, there was no objection to the receiving of Holy Communion. The rubric, then, is seen to be disciplinary and closely resembles Archbishop Peckham's regulation of 1281 against the 'damnable negligence' of those who did not ensure the Confirmation of their children. In both cases the concern was to protect the rite of Confirmation. The rite was seen as important in the life of the member of the Church, and, lest it be neglected, Communion became the bait on the hook of Confirmation. It might be argued that the effect was to devalue and certainly to mistake the nature of Holy Communion and

Confirmation. Confirmation became, in the minds of most, the rite of admission to Holy Communion. Communion became the prize at the end of the course; it is not surprising that for many it should seem to tarnish, rather than to supply spiritual food for the members of Christ's Body. On the other hand, we do well to understand the concern reflected in Peckham's regulation and the rubric. Concerning his own diocese's experience of admission to Communion before Confirmation, the Bishop of Christchurch, New Zealand, wrote in 1982:

> . . . . . In most parishes where the Alternative Practice holds, there is good life and enthusiastic Confirmation, although as you might expect, greatly reduced members. In other parishes, Confirmation has practically died out . . . . .[4]

Even so, to make of Confirmation a hurdle before Communion needs more than the maintenance of discipline as a justification.

That, in certain circumstances, Communion may be received by unconfirmed persons makes very doubtful the conclusion of the 1938 Doctrine Report that in normal circumstances admission to Communion should be founded upon the prior reception of the gift of the Holy Spirit.

> It is evidently appropriate that the rite wherein the gift of the Holy Spirit is bestowed in its fullness should normally preceed admission to participation in the rite which expresses the completeness of Church-membership and of its obligations.[5]

But why only 'normally'? Moreover, is Confirmation 'the rite wherein the gift of the Holy Spirit is bestowed in its fullness'? Notwithstanding the last hundred years of argument, the BCP may prove a truer guide to the tradition we have received. If the Eucharist 'expresses the completeness of Church-membership and of its obligations', does it not therefore relate to Baptism rather than Confirmation?

Baptism and the gift of the Spirit. The 39 Articles and the BCP acknowledge no distinction with regard to the work of the Holy Spirit so that he may, for example, be perceived as externally active in Baptism for the remission of sins, and coming in Confirmation to indwell the individual. Rather, their references must be taken as indicating the fullness of his action in Baptism. Thus, for Article XXVII, in Baptism the promises not only of the forgiveness of sin but also 'of our adoption to be the sons of God by the Holy Ghost, are visibly signed and sealed'. Taking this clear reference to *Romans 8,* it is difficult to envisage a more complete relation of the individual to the Holy Spirit than is here indicated as arising from

Baptism. Within the BCP Order of Public Baptism, the priest 'beseeches the people,

> to call upon God the Father, through our Lord Jesus Christ, that of his bounteous mercy he will grant to this Child that thing which by nature he cannot have, that he may be baptized with water, and the Holy Ghost . . . . .'

Explicitly, after praying for the child's sanctification 'with the Holy Ghost' and the 'remission of his sins by spiritual Regeneration', the Minister goes on to pray,

> Give thy Holy Spirit to this infant, that he may be born again and made an heir of everlasting Salvation . . . . .

It is difficult to imagine that the gift of the Spirit could be any more complete than it is in Baptism. This is borne out by reference to the Baptism 'of such as are of riper years'. The same theology of Baptism underlies this adult order which, like the infant rite, is to be followed by Confirmation. Even though Confirmation might follow within a short time, it is explicitly stated that the Spirit is given in Baptism, particularly in the use of *John 3* at the Gospel, and in the emphasis put upon *Acts 2. 38*

> Doubt ye not . . . . . that he will grant them remission of their sins, and bestow upon them the Holy Ghost.

Finally, BCP rite of Confirmation affirms the work of the Spirit in Baptism. Already, the first prayer declares, God has 'vouchsafed to regenerate these servants by Water and the Holy Ghost'. The Spirit whose work is sought in Confirmation is not being given for the first time. This is quite clear in the change from the prayer of the 1549 rite:

> Send down from heaven we beseech thee (O Lord) upon them thy Holy Ghost the comforter, with the manifold gifts of grace . . . . .

(a request for a new work, taken from the Gelasian Sacramentary,) to the words of 1552 which provide the content of the prayer in the 1662 Order:

> Strengthen them, we beseech thee, O Lord, with the Holy Ghost the Comforter; and *daily increase* in them thy manifold gifts of grace . . . . .

The work of the Spirit has already begun in Baptism. It is not that Confirmation completes that work; rather Confirmation is looked to for a continuing and increasing gift which characterises the life of the Christian. The 'fullness' of the Spirit, then, is given in Baptism.

Admission to Communion requires that fullness, but cannot be argued as being consequent upon Confirmation.

Baptism, membership of the Church, and entry into the Kingdom

> . . . . . my Baptism, wherein I was made a member of Christ, the child of God, and an inheritor of the kingdom of heaven. (The Catechism)

The priest's introduction to the order of Public Baptism refers to baptism 'with water and the Holy Ghost' as the sole means of entry into the Kingdom of God, and also as the means of reception into 'Christ's holy Church'. The implications, however, for participation in the Eucharist are not followed through. The use in the Order for Infant Baptism of *Mark 10. 13 ff* need not of itself justify the Baptism of children. Yet it certainly points to the child as a model for those who would enter the Kingdom. Repeatedly the Baptism rite emphasises that it confers membership of the heavenly kingdom. For this reason it is necessary that children be baptised. When, therefore, the Eucharist is referred to as the 'heavenly Feast',[6] the eschatological act sustaining us until the great banquet of the King, we may ask if children may consistently be excluded. Similarly, in Baptism the individual is made a 'lively member' of the Church. How, though, can he have life in him if he does not 'eat the flesh of the Son of Man and drink his blood' (*John 6. 53 ff*)? And, as we have seen, Cyprian had argued that if *John 3. 5* concerning the need for Baptism was to be applied to children, then no less should *John 6. 53 ff.* Indeed in what sense are those 'that receive Baptism rightly . . . . . grafted into the Church' (Article XXVII) and what does it mean to say 'We receive this child into the Congregation of Christ's flock . . . . .', if we do not accept those baptised into the fellowship of the other sacrament? The question of infant Communion was not a question that concerned the authors of the Prayer Book. Even when it was raised in the seventeenth century, it had its origin in an attack on the practice of infant Baptism,[7] rather than in any positive argument for infant Communion, and was brushed aside at the Restoration. The weight of traditional practice precluded its ever being a real issue. The practice of infant Communion in the ancient Church was known, but that it should have ceased seemed to the Reformers a good enough reason not to consider it. Thus in the *Consultation* of Hermann of Cologne, itself an important source in the compilation of the Prayer Book:

> The old fathers administered this sacrament of the supper of the Lord even to

infants with baptism. But seeing that the custom is worn away not without a cause . . . . .[8]

In fact, no cause is given. What we do see explicitly in the *Consultation* and throughout the Reformation understanding of the place of children in the Church is a biological model of growth. Thus the *Consultation* recommends Baptism in the context of the Eucharist, on the grounds that each sacrament is suitable for the stage which children and parents respectively have reached:

. . . . . they ask and receive the Communion of Christ in Baptism with true faith, they cannot but ask the same for themselves and receive it desirously being offered in the sacrament of Christ's body and blood.[9]

The silence of the tradition concerning infant Communion is, then, the result of the inherited understanding. The Anglican understanding of Baptism, especially concerning the 'membership' it confers, has implications which in the present circumstances need to be worked out afresh.

Baptism and faith. The Reformation emphasis upon the necessity and centrality of faith as that which alone make man's work acceptable to God left its mark upon the Anglican view of the sacrament.[10] In Article XXIX we may perceive a survival of the medieval concern which led to the exclusion of children from Communion until such time as they could be considered able to distinguish the Host from ordinary food, together with an emphasis on the need for faith:

The wicked, and such as be void of a lively faith, although they do carnally and visibly press with their teeth . . . . . the Sacrament of the Body and Blood of Christ, yet in no wise are they partakers of Christ: but rather, to their condemnation, do eat and drink the sign or sacrament of so great a thing.

We shall have cause later to consider the separate question of 'worthy reception'. For now, we may ask whether lack of faith on the part of infants is a cause for keeping them from Communion. Certainly Article XXVIII affirms,

. . . . . the mean whereby the Body of Christ is received and eaten in the Supper is Faith.

This 'Faith' appears in the Catechism necessarily to be of an active nature:

What is required of them who come to the Lord's Supper? To examine themselves, whether they repent them truly of their former sins, stedfastly purposing to lead a new life, have a lively Faith in God's mercy through

> Christ, with a thankful remembrance of his death, and be in Charity with all men.

Such an active faith would seem more than can be expected in an infant. Yet infants could be baptised despite similar requirements laid down for Baptism. In particular the Catechism spoke of the need for

> Repentance, whereby they forsake sin; and faith whereby they stedfastly believe the promises of God made to them in that Sacrament.

Faith, after Luther, was of central importance. Yet he himself had given a clue as to how children may rightly be baptised where faith is essential to meet the divine promise upon which salvation depends:

> On this matter I agree with anyone in saying that infants are helped by vicarious faith: the faith of those who present them for Baptism. The word of God, whenever uttered, is powerful enough to change the hearts even of the ungodly, and these are not less unresponsive and incapable than any infant. Further, all things are possible in response to the prayers of a believing church when it presents the infant, and this is changed, cleansed and renewed, by their infused faith.[11]

This understanding was reflected in the Catechism in its question and answer:

> Why then are infants baptized, when by reason of their tender age they cannot perform them? (i.e. the requirements of repentance and faith) Because they promise them both by their sureties: which promise, when they come to age, themselves are bound to perform.

If the faith of others could supply what was necessary for baptismal faith, we may ask if the lack of personal faith should be any objection to the reception of Communion by infants, particularly when their Baptism declaredly makes them 'lively members' of the Church.

Difficulties in the extension of Communion to the unconfirmed, implicit in the nature of the Baptismal rite

The vicarious nature of baptismal faith. The argument of the previous section has been that if the faith of the Church declared by sponsors suffices for Baptism, then there is no reason why it should not suffice for the reception of Communion. But there is a further emphasis on the need for a personal profession of faith. While this need not be regarded as a conclusive argument against infant and child Communion, it deserves brief mention. It cannot be made to apply to those baptised as adults who speak for themselves. The effect of promises made in Baptism by godparents is to 'bind' the children by them:

> Dost thou not think that thou art bound to believe and to do as they have promised for thee?
> Yea verily: and by God's help so I will . . . . .
> And I pray unto God to give me his grace,
> that I may continue in the same unto my life's end.

The binding of which the Catechism speaks is absolute. Faith, then, must already be active in the Baptism of the child who is made regenerate and enjoys the full status of a 'member of Christ' (Catechism) who is 'grafted into the Church' (Article XXVII). Yet there is also an idea that more remains to be done. The continuing grace may, no doubt, be supplied in a variety of ways of which Confirmation is but one. But Confirmation had come to have a pivotal role in matters of faith and grace. Largely retaining the medieval biological model for the administration of the sacraments, the BCP continued the tradition that it was at the age of discretion that new sources of grace were necessary for the individual; regardless of what was started in Baptism, to petition in Confirmation specifically for 'strengthening' and 'an increase' of grace was to imply that these hitherto had not been necessary. Thus, what was given in Baptism found in Confirmation a definite stage in the unfolding of the gift. Similarly with regard to faith. The faith of sponsors had so far sufficed. It was as binding as baptismal grace was indelible. Yet it needed an unfolding in personal affirmation. Thus the Catechism, speaking of the baptismal faith professed by godparents in the name of the child, continued:

> . . . . . which promise, when they come to Age, themselves are bound to perform.

The faith of the Church had to be made the faith of the individual. And with the 1662 Book, 'Confirmation' received a new meaning, referring not only to the grace conferred, but concerning the renewal of baptismal vows:

> ratifying and confirming the same in your own persons, and acknowledging yourselves bound to believe and to do all these things which your Godfathers and Godmothers then undertook for you.

Personal faith, then, had to be declared. This was appropriate at the age of discretion, until which age grace additional to that of Baptism was not considered necessary. In this way Confirmation became fixed as the means of admission to Communion.

The social nature of Baptism. Halfway through the century of Prayer Book revision, Richard Hooker could write:

> ..... there is not any man of the Church of England but the same man is also a member of the commonwealth; not any man a member of the commonwealth which is not also a member of the Church of England.[12]

As the Church of the Nation, the Church of England welcomed into membership by Baptism all who were brought to it. According to Canon LXVII of the Canons of 1604,

> No Minister shall refuse or delay to christen any child ..... that is brought to the Church to him upon Sundays or Holy Days to be christened ..... convenient warning being given him thereof before, in such manner and form as is prescribed in the ..... Book of Common Prayer.

Even today, Canon B22 forbids any refusal or delay to baptise any infant within a minister's cure, 'save for the purpose of preparing or instructing the parents or guardians or godparents'. Where there is a more evident difference between the 1604 and the 1969 Canons is in the provision of sanctions concerning those who sought Baptism. In today's Church, encouragement, exhortation and nagging are the only means available in seeking the fulfilment of baptismal responsibilities. The 1604 Canons order the 'present'-ing of non-communicants (LXII and LXLV) and provide penalties against both clergy and those responsible for children and others who fail in their duties concerning catechesis. Nor are the sanctions merely legal. Canon XXIV required that godparents be communicants:

> ..... neither shall any person be admitted Godfather or Godmother to any Child at Christening or Confirmation, before the said person so undertaking have received the Holy Communion.

The present Canon B23 seeks godparents,

> who will faithfully fulfil their responsibilities both by their care for the children committed to their charge and by the example of their own godly living.

The place of Confirmation in Christian Initiation

The Reformers made of Confirmation something quite other than it had previously been. Already we have seen how its necessity as a sacrament conferring the new gift of the Spirit had been denied. Here we may turn to the positive merits with which it was attributed.

Confirmation in the BCP received the alternative title, 'Laying on of hands upon those that are baptised and come to years of discretion'. This in itself was significant, representing a conscious move to a rite which required understanding on the part of the candidate, as opposed to the medieval rites which came to coincide with the age of discretion but, until the Counter-Reformation, did not examine the faith of the candidate. In making this change, Cranmer and other reformers saw themselves returning to a more ancient practice. His preface to *The Catechism of Justus Jonas* drew out the value of Confirmation in 'the education of the youth', which value gained explicit recognition in the coupling of the learning of the Catechism with and as a pre-condition of Confirmation. As he wrote in the preface to the first-mentioned Catechism, there would be no need for so many laws, injunctions and proclamations,

> if so great negligence of the education of youth had not been so much suffered, and the necessary points and articles of our religion and profession omitted . . . . .
>
> . . . . . or if the ancient and laudable ceremony of Confirmation had continued in the old state . . . . . where an exact and strait examination was had of all such as were of full age, both of their professions that they made in baptism touching their belief and keeping of God's commandments, with a general solemn rehearsal of the said commandments and of all the articles of faith . . . . .[13]

For the Prayer Book of 1549 and 1552, the rite was 'agreeable with the usage of the Church in times past'. Its use for those 'of perfect age', its requirement of instruction, open profession of faith and promise of obedience to God's will were all taken to be 'ordained'. That it was not in fact 'ordained' makes it no less a part of the tradition. It fulfilled what was considered necessary for the adolescent; particularly in instruction. The prayer for grace and strength may be given more than one interpretation. The rubric of 1549 and 1552 did not reappear in 1662; namely, that by virtue of the strength given, 'it is most mete to be ministered when children come to that age, yet partly by the frailty of their own flesh, partly by the assaults of the world and the Devil, they begin to be in danger to fall into sundry kinds of sin'.[14] Moreover, though the language implied its use with adolescents (e.g. 'to the end that children being now come to the years of discretion . . . . .'), it gave a place for the personal profession of faith which all previous unreformed rites had lacked.

It is as a rite for those able to profess their faith that Confirmation has its value in the Anglican tradition. It was necessary, not because by its own instrinsic nature it conferred a gift otherwise lacking, but because of what the Church willed to make it. To propose to make Confirmation an integral part of the Baptism of infants is therefore unacceptable: the grace conferred is received only in connection with the profession of faith. Thus it is ordered by the Church that candidates shall 'openly before the Church ratify and confirm' their baptismal promises. Nor is it acceptable to make of Confirmation merely a commitment or renewal of promises. Rather the 'ratifying and confirming' by the candidates is done before the Bishop whose prayer, made in the congregation, with the imposition of hands itself confirms that faith. Confirmation is a two-part rite and neither part may stand alone. Furthermore, the necessity of Confirmation relates to the Church's self-understanding and the position of its members.

This is expressed in the collect said by the Bishop:

> ..... We make our humble supplications unto thee for these thy servants, upon whom (after the example of thy Holy Apostles) we have now laid our hands to certify them (by this sign) of thy favour and gracious goodness towards them .....

It is the idea of 'certifying' faith which would seem central.

As has been mentioned, the rubrics concerning Confirmation made it the pre-condition of admission to Communion. How far this should guide us now is open to discussion, for there is no necessity in them.

The work of the Spirit in Confirmation is also discussed above, as a strengthening and increase of a gift already given. The confirmatory prayers themselves may best be taken as relating to the work of the Spirit in the whole Church. 'The spirit of wisdom and understanding .....' etc. are the attributes of the Isaianic Messiah, and here the messianic community prays for their increase in one who by Baptism is a member of the Church. In Cranmer's words at the Consecration of 1537:

> The Bishop in the name of Church doth invocate the Holy Ghost to give strength and constancy with other spiritual gifts unto the person confirmed, so that the efficiency of this sacrament is of such value as is the prayer of the Bishop made in the name of the Church.[15]

Finally in this section, the close connection of the Catechism with the Confirmation rite, as a pre-condition in 1662, and part of the rite itself in 1549 and 1552 is an important reminder of the importance attributed to understanding that faith must be alive.

The Eucharist and the issue of worthy reception
In the same way that the Church treated Baptism as the sacrament of infancy, so the Eucharist was seen as the sacrament for adult spiritual nourishment. The result is that even the 1662 order failed properly to tackle the question of the standing in the Church of those baptised in adulthood, and nowhere is the need seen to treat children as worthy or unworthy with regard to the reception of Holy Communion. Reference to infant Communion tended to spring from other arguments with neither party wanting it. Baptists raised it as coeval with infant Baptism. The Jesuit, Harding, raised it in connection with the issue of Communion in both kinds, arguing with Jewel that the command 'Drink this *all* of you' should be interpreted as a command to priests only. If Jewel wished to interpret 'all' literally then he must include young children and infants to whom the primitive Church gave the chalice.[16]

To Jewel has been attributed Homily XV, 'Of the worthy receiving and reverent esteeming of the Sacrament of the Body and Blood of Christ'. From the start, the Homily treats the sacrament as relating to the adult consciousness and need:

> . . . . . being rightly done by the faithful, it doth not only help their weakness, who be by their poisoned nature readier to remember injuries than benefits, but strengtheneth and comforteth their inward man with peace and gladness.

The categories in which the Reformation writers treat the question of reception are almost always those which will apply to adults. If, for example, the conscience is to be searched and examined before receiving Communion (First Exhortation, 1662 Holy Communion), is the infant or child disqualified through inability to do so? What is 'reverence' when it is asked of a child? Or 'ignorance', when it is condemned? The issue is not merely one of what makes the individual culpable, so excluding a child in his innocence. The Fifteenth Homily declared,

> . . . . . we must certainly know that three things be requisite in him which would seemly resort to the Lord's table: that is, a right and a worthy estimation and understanding of this mystery; secondly to come in a sure faith; and thirdly to have newness or pureness of life to succeed the receiving of the same.

A child could have none of these as a personal quality; but could they be supplied in the way that the repentance and faith necessary for Baptism were supplied by the godparents' sureties? So it has been argued, but it must be said that the tradition of the times treats the faith and other qualities necessary for worthy reception of Communion from a more individualistic stance. In Baptism the child is grafted into the Church by the Church's faith, declared by the godparents. At the Eucharist, it is only by faith that the individual can perceive the benefits he receives. This may be drawn out thus:

The Eucharist and 'remembrance':
..... every one of us must be guests and not gazers, eaters and not lookers, feeding ourselves and not hiring others to feed for us ..... of necessity we must be ourselves partakers of this table.

The implications from this part of the homily might seem to be that all who are present at the Eucharist should receive Communion. For us, when we encourage the attendance of children, that may be the case. For Jewel, however, in making the Eucharist analogous to the Passover what was important is that what it represents be understood:

> ..... as of old time God decreed his wondrous benefits of the deliverance of his people to be kept *in memory* by the eating of the Passover with his rites and ceremonies, so our Loving Saviour hath ordained and established the *remembrance* of his great mercy expressed in his passion in the institution of the Lord's Supper.

At the Lord's Table, it is 'not only the rites and ceremonies of his Passover, but the cause and end thereon ..... which must be taught to God's people's posterity'.

Reception and receptionism: The doctrine of the Eucharist expressed in the BCP required a faith built upon understanding if, in Jewel's words, it was to be more than 'a bare sign, no untrue figure of a thing absent'. The words of the Prayer of Humble Access indicate that, more than eating and drinking, it is the manner of doing so which is important:

> *so* to eat ..... and to drink ..... that our sinful bodies may be made clean by his body and our souls washed through his most precious blood .....

More than table-fellowship is required by Jewel's Fifteenth Homily. He sees

> no warm ceremony ..... but the table of the Lord, the bread and cup of the Lord, the memory of Christ the annunciation of his death, yea, the communion of the body and blood of the Lord in a marvellous incorporation, which by the operation of the Holy Ghost ..... *is through faith wrought in the souls of the faithful.* Such a food must be thirsted for; not as specially regarding

> the terrene and earthly creatures which remain, but always holding fast and cleaving to the Rock whence we may suck the sweetness of everlasting salvation.

Discernment, then, is central to Eucharistic doctrine, as well as active will and memory.

The Eucharist and 'learners in religion':
Jewel's reference to the exclusion of penitents and catechumens from the Eucharist of the primitive Church on the grounds that 'this table receiveth no unholy, unclean or sinful guests' cannot be applied directly to children who, although learners, differ by their Baptism. Yet there is a evident concern that those who have not professed the faith publicly may be unworthy. Behind Cranmer's emphasis on belief lies the assumption that only this will bring peace and order. To be ignorant was to be in a state which needed remedying, hence the emphasis of the 1604 Canons on the Catechism. Bucer illustrates the concern that any lack of understanding may be culpable:

> ..... it is evident that not a few children make a confession of this kind (Confirmation) with no more understanding of the faith than some parrot uttering his hello.[17]

Bucer wanted first to see the fruits of the Spirit, for:

> in every administration of the holy things of Christ, care must be taken that some holy thing of the Lord is not thrown to the dogs, and that the pearls of the Kingdom of Christ are not scattered to the swine .....

Where such sentiments prevailed, we may perhaps ask why those who could approach the Table needed to say, 'We are not worthy so much as to gather up the crumbs under thy Table'?

---

[1] The issues concerning Christian Initiation and discussed at the Savoy Conference may be found e.g. in C.E. Pocknee: *Confirmation in the Anglican Tradition* (CQR Vol. 167 No. 363 pp. 72ff), an article with little enthusiasm for ecumenism.

[2] Cranmer's answers are to be found in J.D.C. Fisher, *Christian Initiation, the Reformation Period,* pp. 223ff.

[3] From the title and opening rubrics of the rite, first introduced in 1662. The criticism has been made that the rite's baptismal theology was insufficiently removed from the understanding that Baptism was a rite for infants. But the order does recognise the ability of the candidates to answer for themselves, their instruction precedes Baptism rather than Confirmation, and it will be argued that the rite of Confirmation was

[4] Letter of the Rt Rev. W.A. Pyatt to the Rev. Barry Miller, Board of Education, 23rd June, 1982.

[5] (*The Report of the Commission on Christian Doctrine* appointed by the Archbishops of Canterbury and York in 1922), p. 189.
[6] The first exhortation at Holy Communion (1662).
[7] See Holeton, op. cit. pp.16ff.
[8] in Fisher . . . *Reformation* op cit. p.57.
[9] *Ibid.* p.56.
[10] Article VII.
[11] Luther, *Babylonian Captivity*, in Fisher: *Reformation* op. cit., pp.4f.
[12] cited in P.R. Cornwell's working paper, *Christian Initiation*, GS 184.
[13] Fisher, op. cit., p.235.
[14] *Prayer Book of 1549, 1552,* Confirmation, opening rubrics.
[15] Fisher, op. cit., p.219.
[16] J.M.M Dalby, *The End of Infant Communion* CQR Vol. 167 No. 36 p.6.
[17] Censura–Fisher, op. cit., pp. 244–8.

Appendix 5 Confirmation Statistics

Confirmations in Age Groups

Year	Under 12	12–15	16–19	Totals
1970	15,138	66,439	8,358	89,935
1971	14,710	64,570	8,120	87,400
1972	14,636	62,019	8,497	85,152
1973	17,039	56,709	7,412	81,160
1974	17,348	53,179	7,125	77,652
1975	16,873	53,881	6,910	77,664
1976	16,518	51,016	7,768	75,302
1977	15,540	50,781	9,042	75,363
1978	15,563	50,939	8,834	75,336
1979	15,131	48,701	8,940	72,772
1980	15,536	49,051	7,627	72,214
1981	14,978	42,776	7,532	65,286
1982	14,157	39,878	6,289	60,324
Totals	203,167	689,939	102,454	995,560

The total number confirmed 1970–1982 under the age of 20 was 995,560. In 1970 there were 1,814,000 Easter Communicants. By 1982 we could expect 1,320,000 of these still to be alive. So we could estimate a potential Easter Communicants figure for 1982 of about 2,316,000. The actual number of Easter Communicants in 1982 was 1,674,000, about 642,000 lower than the potential figure, or, expressing this as a percentage of the potential figure, about 28% lower.

NOTES ON CONFIRMATION STATISTICS

The figure of 2,316,000 potential Easter Communicants can only be taken as a rough guide.

It is likely to underestimate the true figure for the following reasons:

(a) Not all those confirmed before 1970 will be included in the 1970 Easter Communicants figure.

(b) Those confirmed aged 20 and over are not included.

It is possible that the figure may overestimate for the following reason:

(c) A zero death-rate has been assumed for those confirmed 1970–1982.

The following factors may also influence the final figure:

(d) It is assumed that the 1970 Easter Communicants all fall into the 40 and over age group. Hence the death-rate which has been applied is for the over 40s.

(e) The death-rate has been calculated for the population of England and Wales, whereas the Easter Communicants are virtually all resident in England.

(f) It is not possible to make any adjustments for the social class of church members, since there is no source data.

(g) The death-rate used throughout is based on figures for 1982.

(h) No adjustment has been made for immigration/emigration.

(i) Figures for H.M. Forces arc not included.

(j) Some of those confirmed in 1970 (i.e., before Easter) will be included in the 1970 Easter Communicant figure. Those confirmed in 1982 after Easter may not be included in the 1982 Communicant figures.

(Figures supplied by Statistics Department of the Central Board of Finance.)

Bibliography

AUTHOR	TITLE	PUBLISHER	DATE
Archbishops' Commission on Christian Doctrine	*The Report of the Commission on Christian Doctrine: Doctrine in the Church of England*		1938
Aries, P.,	*Centuries of Childhood*	Penguin	1973
Berger, P.,	*The Social Reality of Religion*	Faber & Faber	1969
Bocock, R.,	*Ritual in Industrial Society*	George Allen & Unwin	1974
British Council of Churches,	*The Child in the Church*	BCC	1976
British Council of Churches,	*Understanding Christian Nurture*	BCC	1981
Church Information Office	*The Alternative Service Book 1980. A Commentary by the Liturgical Commission*	CIO	1980
Church of Scotland, Department of Education	*Children at the Table*	Church of Scotland	1982
Cornwell, R.P.,	*Christian Initiation*	GS 184	
Dalby, J.M.M.,	*The End of Infant Communion*		
Dulles, SJ.A.,	*Models of the Church*	Gill & MacMillan	1974
Fisher, J.D.C.,	*Christian Initiation: Baptism in the Medieval West*	SPCK/AC	1965
	Christian Initiation—the Reformation Period	AC/SPCK	1970
	Confirmation. Then and Now	AC/SPCK	1978
Fowler, J.W.,	*Stages of Faith*	Harper & Row	1981
General Synod,	*Christian Initiation: Birth and Growth in the Christian Society. The Ely Report*	CIO, GS 30	1971
General Synod Board of Education,	*Coming In*	CIO	1977

AUTHOR	TITLE	PUBLISHER	DATE
Goffman, E.,	*Asylums*	Doubleday Anchor	1961
Holeton, D.,	*Infant Communion—then and now*	Grove Liturgical Study 27	1961
Klapp, O.,	*Collective Search for Identity*	Holt, Rinehart, Winston Inc.	1969
Lucas, W.,	*The Christian Approach to Non-Christian Customs in Christianity and Native Rites*	UMCA	1928
Martin, D.,	*A General Theory of Secularisation*	Blackwell	1978
Mead, M.,	*Coming of Age in Samoa*	Penguin	1928 & 1963
Moran, G.,	*Religious Education Development*	Winston Press	1983
Perry, M.	*Crisis for Confirmation*	SCM Press	1967
Pocknee, C.E.,	*Confirmation in the Anglican Tradition*	CQR	
Sheehy, G.,	*Passages*	Bantam Books	1977
Turner, B.,	*Religion and Social Theory*	Heinemann	1983
Turner, V.,	*The Ritual Process*	Routledge & Kegan Paul	1969
Van Gennep, A.,	*Rites de Passage*	Routledge & Kegan Paul	1960
Wadderton Group, The,	*Alive in God's World Series*	CIO	1968/9
Westerhoff, J.H.,	*Will Our Children Have Faith?*	Seabury Press	1976
Westerhoff and Willimon,	*Liturgy and Learning through the Life Cycles*	Seabury Press	1980

AUTHOR	TITLE	PUBLISHER	DATE
Wilson, B.,	*Patterns of Sectarianism. Organisation and Ideology in Social and Religious Movements*	Heinemann	1967
	Religion in Sociological Perspective	Oxford University Press	1982
World Council of Churches,	*Ecumenical Perspectives on Baptism, Eucharist and Ministry*	Faith and Order Paper no. 116	1983
	Baptism, Eucharist and Ministry	Faith and Order Paper no. 111	1982
	Ecumenical Perspectives on Baptism, Eucharist and Ministry	Faith and Order Paper no. 116	1983
	..... *and do not hinder them*	Faith and Order Paper no. 109	
Yinger, M.,	*The Scientific Study of Religion*	Macmillan	1970
Young, D.,	*Welcoming Children to Communion*	Grove Worship series no. 85	1983